MW01258920

Calluses and Character:

The Life and Times of a Kentucky Sharecropper

By Kenneth Croslin

Old Seventy Creek Press 2011

This book is dedicated to the memory of my father and mother who gave so much and to my sisters, Jeanne and Elizabeth, and my brothers, Buddy and Robert. I also dedicate it to Barbara, Billy, Tommy, Wanda, Glenn and Steve. I especially dedicate it to my wife, Linda who has stood by me all these years and to our children, Amy, Jeff, and Kevin, who have been so helpful and supportive!

2011 **Old Seventy Creek Press**
First Edition
Printed In the United States of America
All Rights reserved under international
and Pan-American Copyright Conventions

Published in the United States
by: Old Seventy Creek Press
      Rudy Thomas, Publisher
      P. O. box 204
      Albany, Kentucky 42602

ISBN: 978-0615564227 (Old Seventy Creek Press)
EAN: 0615564224

Acknowledgments

I wish to acknowledge Byron Crawford for his support of my work at *Kentucky Living* magazine and for his foreword to this collection.

I also wish to acknowledge my son, Kevin R. Croslin, for writing the introduction to this first edition of my collected stories.

I wish to acknowledge my daughter, Amy Wright, for proof reading the manuscript.

I also wish to acknowledge Lavena Baier and Leann Ballard, the copyright holders of all the images taken by Sister's Creations Photography located at 3747 Randolph Road, Edmonton, Kentucky who so graciously granted their copyright release of images titled: **Kenneth Croslin 2011.**

Calluses and Character
Foreword by Byron Crawford

You have opened a very special collection of stories between the covers of Kenneth Croslin's first book.

In fact, you are about to read many pages lifted from intensely personal moments of Croslin's life as the second youngest of 11 children of a southern Kentucky farm couple from his father's birth in 1910 to 2010. One hundred years of his family's history are covered, a smile and a tear at a time.

Books have been written about every subject imaginable, but far too few about the lives of sharecropper families, which were a corner post of Kentucky's farm culture through much of the early to mid-20th Century, as America dug itself out of the Great Depression and the war years.

Croslin's *Calluses and Character* is a rich tapestry of love, humor, hard work, hardship, perseverance and honesty, which characterized his and his siblings' growing up years.

I had only to read two or three of Croslin's stories to realize that he had seen and vividly remembered what many others either missed or perhaps could not put into words.

His poignant story about his school picture was so moving that I asked his permission to use excerpts in my back page in *Kentucky Living* magazine, where it elicited many compliments and requests for a book of his works from among *Kentucky Living's* million plus readers.

One of Croslin's great gifts is that he is more a professional storyteller than a professional writer, and is able to relate memories so straight from the heart in such a clear and direct manner that those who open his book may sense more that they are listening to his voice than reading his words.

His book belongs in any classroom in which Kentucky's 20th Century culture is being studied.

If you were born to one of the many hard-working farm families in Kentucky during the early-to-mid-1900s, you may find that Kenneth Croslin has captured some of your life moments in these pages. If you were not, then you will finish this book with a better understanding of, and appreciation for, a remarkable generation of Kentucky farmers whose lives and labors served as a lasting template for Croslin's *Calluses and Character.*

Good Reading,
Byron Crawford—
Kentucky Living

Byron Crawford, courtesy of KET

Calluses and Character
Introduction

I learned a great deal growing up in rural Kentucky. Lots of things have changed in the world around me since then. However, one thing that has always remained constant is the values and lessons learned from my father, Kenneth Croslin.

His book, *Calluses and Character*, is a compilation of all the stories I loved hearing growing up, and even some that I had not heard. Written about his life and the lives of his family members, Dad gives the reader a bird's eye view of a world where hard work meant the difference between eating or starving. Government assistance was minimal and that was the way his folks wanted it. They had pride. They had togetherness, and most importantly they had love.

My Dad is the kind of man that lives by his word. He taught us all that a good name is worth more than possessions. Hard work can always be relied on to see you through hard times, and lying and cheating will only make matters worse.

The stories in this book are not your typical hard living stories. They are stories that bear witness to how love, laughter, and a good strong moral foundation can triumph over heartache and leave a person with sense of peace and accomplishment even in the darkest and most trying times in our lives. This book makes me proud to be a Croslin.

Kevin R. Croslin

Prologue

I started thinking about writing a book about my parents and family a few years back but it was kind of like one of those old fifty watt bulbs used to do during a thunder storm--it would come and go. Well, I have come to realize that my time to do this is getting shorter with each passing year, so this is my feeble attempt to put onto paper some of the things my family experienced while growing up poor here in Kentucky. We were poor only in that we never had much money, never owned any property while my father was alive, and never gained importance in the communities we lived in, beyond that of being good neighbors, trustworthy, and hardworking, honest people. We were not much different from most of the folks we knew, because there just wasn't much wealth to be found among rural Kentuckians but for just a few exceptions. I guess you could say we lived in our own little world, and that's not all that bad come to think of it. There have been times in my own personal life that "our own little world" sure seemed safe and secure in comparison.

Kentucky was a perfect place for poor people to live. You could grow a vegetable garden just about anywhere. The woods and fields were teeming with wild game for meat, and the streams were loaded with fish of just about every species. I've heard my brother Tommy laugh and tell people that we ate so many ground hogs, he could look at one's track and tell you how many potatoes it would take to cook with it. Of course he was joking a little bit, but only just a little. Before the advent of bush hog mowers, every cow pasture flat and fence row would be loaded with blackberries. I remember my family picking blackberries to can and to sell to the folks in town that had money. It wasn't really hard work, but it sure did get hot in those briar patches. And the chiggers would absolutely eat you up. Chiggers were a tiny little red insect only a little bit larger than a germ that would bury into your skin and itch like the devil. The more you scratched it the worse it itched. We used to say you could kill one chigger and a million would come to his funeral The only way to repel them in those days was with coal oil. This was what we called kerosene. We would soak a rag in coal oil and just brush it around lightly on our clothes, shoes, and skin. I guess the Croslin family smelled like a truck stop when we left the house to pick blackberries.

My parents never talked politics too much. Maybe they just felt that whatever decisions were made it would have meant little change for sharecroppers and other poor folks like us, but they always found a way to get to the polls and vote. I don't think they ever had to walk to the polls, but if not having a ride there meant they would miss voting they would have walked. I believe all their children vote every time there is an election.

I was almost twelve years old when Daddy died, and sometimes it's hard to remember exactly what he looked like. But I will never forget his voice. He was a wonderful story teller and loved a joke better than anybody I ever knew. I think every one of his children inherited that quality from him. People have always said I was full of it, and so was he. They also said the same things about every one of his kids at one time or another. He loved to play with us and was almost always in a good mood, but when he told you to do something you had best not have to be told twice. He would not tolerate any of us talking back or sassing him or Momma. We were taught to be mannerly with everyone. You never, ever called an older person by their first names. It was Mr. and Mrs. The only exceptions were very close family friends. It's funny but I always thought the Talleys were kin to us. All I had ever heard my older brothers and sisters call them was Uncle Jacob and Aunt Leara.

When we were in school, there was order and control. Unlike schools today, if a student crossed over the line, the teacher would deliver the punishment. Usually no more than a light spanking where the embarrassment hurt much more than the slap on the bottom. I'm amazed today at the tolerance level of parents. For instance, I've seen kids at the local super store where within three minutes every person in the entire store knew the kid's first name, as in Joey come back here, Joey put that back, Joey leave that alone, Joey stop that please, Joey don't. What Joey needs is a little dose of what we called, "The Phillip Croslin Half a Minute Makeover." About six and up to but no more than ten swats across the rear end with his belt. That would cure Joey of insubordination, be easier on his ears, and Joey's mom's vocal chords and nerves could finally heal. The family harmony would be so much more improved. You see, there is a real difference between love and respect and our parents received both and gave both. They weren't tyrants, just parents that loved their kids and we loved them. We were never promised a whipping. If we needed it we got it right then and it was over and done with but not soon forgotten by us! If we disagreed with Daddy on how something should be done, we always gave him the benefit of the doubt and did it his way. Reason being there was a fifty-fifty chance he was right and a one hundred percent chance he was the boss. It worked for us!

If Phillip and Julia could be here right now to see how their children, grandchildren, and great grandchildren have turned out, they would be mighty proud. At this writing, the family includes a preacher, teachers, lawyer, doctor, Sunday school teacher, quality manager, salesmen, plumber, finish carpenter, cabinet maker and the list goes on and on! That's pretty incredible come to think of it since neither one of them went beyond the eighth grade in school. It certainly wasn't from a lack of brains, but rather just the times in which they lived. I remember they both thought school was important. But, behaving yourself was even more important to them. Daddy always said, "You might be too dumb to learn anything in school, but you better never come home with a bad conduct grade on your report card." We all took him at his word! I think his philosophy would work to everyone's advantage if it were practiced more today!

Some of the stories in this book may mirror events that happened in the lives of those who read this, since so many of us came from the same type background and conditions. For the most part, I want to relay the joy and fun that only a big family can experience as well as a few of the really tough times and Lord knows we had our share of those. I suppose our ability to laugh in the face of adversity kept the hard times from hurting so bad, and that made the good times we had just that much better. I believe almost any poor person that lived in rural Kentucky in our times could write a book much like this one. I should have done this several years ago, but that would have left out all the things that have happened to us lately. So don't expect to hear any hidden family legends, just some stories about Phillip and Julia and their eleven children. Let me introduce them in order of age: Elizabeth, Jeanne, Barbara, Buddy, Billy, Robert, Tommy, Wanda, Glenn, Kenneth, and Steve.

Every single story you're about to read in this book is true, and the names haven't been changed to protect the guilty or the innocent! When I began writing this book my hands were shaking. I was afraid I wouldn't be able to finish it and if I did finish it, would I get it right? I believe I've gotten it as right as I can, but, I'll let you the reader be the judge of that.

Tough Beginnings
Phillip
1910

My father, Phillip James Croslin, was born
July 2nd, 1910, in Warren County, Kentucky.
Daddy had a rough start in this world. When he
was just a few days old, his mother, Georgia
Richards Croslin, took pneumonia and died.
That happened often in those days when there
weren't any real miracle drugs such as we have
today that could have saved her life. Back in
those days, it was believed a woman should stay
in bed for a couple of weeks after giving birth.
Many women took pneumonia and died because
of this practice and most likely so did Grandma.
My grandfather, Jesse Smith Croslin, a farmer in
Warren County, came into the house to eat
dinner, which is the noontime meal here in
Kentucky, and found my grandmother dead in
bed. It was supposed that Grandma had gone to
lie down with the baby to rest while he nursed,
and that's the way Grandpa found them. Like I
said earlier, that's a rough way to start out in
this world. Daddy had an older sister, Gladys,
who would have been about six at the time their
mother died. There was no way Grandpa could
work making a living on the farm with a
newborn baby to care for at the same time, so a
neighbor family, J.B. and Sarah Wright, took
Daddy in until Grandpa could find a way to care
for him. Aunt Gladys was old enough to stay
with Grandpa. Although she was very young,
she could still stay with her daddy and sort of

look after herself while he farmed. Looking back on it, she probably had a harder time of it than Phillip. How hard that must have been for her as a child to have lost her mother, separated from her brother, and have to assume such a responsibility as taking care of the housework at such a tender age. Life can sure kick your butt for you sometimes through absolutely no fault of your own. In my life time, I don't remember ever seeing a six year old child that was mature enough to do that, but then again tough times can make you grow up in a hurry. I don't really know much about Aunt Gladys, because she married and moved to Illinois long before I was born and I only saw her a very few times at family reunions once in a great while. She seemed to be a very sweet person the best I remember.

Grandpa later remarried and he and his wife had four children together. Daddy loved three of them like they were his full brother and sisters. Daddy never cared much for Mammy Grace as he called his stepmother, and I think the feelings were mutual. Daddy never moved into his father's house to live and he stayed with the Wrights until he and Momma were married.

The Wrights gave Daddy a good stable home. He thought a lot of them and I'm sure he did everything he could for them. This wasn't an isolated incident for there have been several people I have known that were taken in by people outside of their family and raised as if they were their own children. This was done purely out of the goodness of their hearts for there wasn't any money from local agencies like there are now.

Daddy from time to time would get drunk and like a lot of people, his true feelings would surface. When this happened, he would occasionally talk about his mother and how he missed her as a child. Once, when he was pretty well tanked up, he said he was the only man he ever heard of that had nursed a dead woman. Just hearing him say that gave me the chills. He was referring to his mother who had died while lying down with him to rest as he nursed when he was just a few days old. Evidently that tortured him for the rest of his life. He never knew the exact plot at Burton Memorial where she was buried so he couldn't even place flowers on her grave. We never knew why Grandpa never showed him where his mother was buried. Like a lot of the country cemeteries the records were poor if they even existed at all, and Burton Memorial was no different. In 2009 our family had a reunion and we talked about having a memorial stone erected in memory of Daddy's mother. In 2010, we took donations from Daddy's children, grand children, and even great grandchildren and had a very nice memorial erected. It wasn't that we had to take donations. It was just a way to give everybody an opportunity to have a part in it. There was an empty plot right behind Daddy's headstone and we were able to put her stone there. If Grandma were actually buried there, Daddy would be resting at her feet, and I believe he would think that was just fine, maybe even giving him the peace he never found while he was alive. I personally think that was one of the best things we ever did together as a family. While talking with a member of the Burton Memorial cemetery committee, he told me there were over fifty people buried there in unmarked graves. On the way home that day I was thinking how awful it would be to pass through this world, live a life, and die and be buried in an unmarked grave. In just a few short years after your close kin had also passed, you would be lost! There would be no visible record of your ever having been here in this world, unless someone found an obscure recorded entry in the files of the Department of Vital Statistics.

I've often wondered over the years why anyone would have as many children as my Daddy and Momma had. I've come to believe while writing this book that Daddy just wanted somebody to love him. He never felt his own mother's love, the comfort of her arms, a soothing voice when he was sick or hurt, or lonely. A father that didn't love him enough to come for him, that should have come for him and taken him home with him to stay and faced down a wife who treated Daddy badly on the few short visits he did spend with them. That's why he wanted to surround himself with a big family. He wanted someone to love and to be loved by in return. He was hugely successful in that endeavor!

A Knack for Nicks
Phillip
1910-1961

Phillip Croslin was a farmer, a horse and mule trainer, a blacksmith, a jokester, as well as many other things he was noted for being good at doing. One thing however that never made the list was his knack for giving all of us nicknames. Some were well thought out nicks and some were just spur of the moment ones and a few were so ridiculous that Momma would step in and shut down his name factory, at least for a while. Here are some of the stories behind the nicknames he gave us, starting with the oldest. Sarah Elizabeth: "Punch." None of us really remember the back ground for Elizabeth's nickname because she was the oldest child, but then again Daddy never really needed a reason for doing this. He called her "Punch" maybe because she had a great right jab. We just aren't sure about it.

Phyllis Jeanne: "String Bean." Jeanne was pretty tall for a girl, or at least she was tall back in those days. She was about five feet seven inches tall, and skinny as a rail.

Barbara Yvonne: None of us, including Barbara, could remember a nickname for her. We are all certain she had one, but maybe she was fortunate enough to have shaken hers before it became permanently established. When I asked her about it, she did however offer two

fitting choices if I wanted to use them: "Queen" or "Princess." Nah, I don't think so, Sis!
Hugh Wright: "Buddy." Buddy was the first boy after three girls and it's safe to say Daddy planned on him being his little buddy. After Elizabeth was born he wanted his next child to be a boy. He was crazy about the three girls but like most men I'm sure he wanted a boy to carry on the Croslin name.

Billy James: "Jim." Billy had the most sensible nickname of the entire bunch. At least it was a derivative of James and nothing you'd mind being called. Maybe Momma stepped up to the plate here on this one. If so, bless her heart!

Robert Douglas: "Pud" as in pudding. There was a fellow in our neighborhood called Pud Rice and he was a huge man weighing around three hundred pounds. Robert as a small boy was a chubby little guy and Daddy saw a similarity down the road I guess. So he called Robert "Pud."

Thomas Earl: "Pore Boy." Like Jeanne, Tommy was built for speed in his younger days. He was tall as well as being of slender build. Daddy called him Pore Boy because he was slim as a snake. It's a wonder he wasn't called Snake. Whew!

Wanda Louise: "Fat Women." Wanda was a chubby little girl when she was two or three years old so that's where he got her nickname. What's unusual about it was that he pronounced it in the plural tense. Maybe he wanted twins. Who knows?

Glenn Ray: "Pomp." This is an easy one. Back in the forties there was an old black man named Pomp Hayes who was a horse trader. Every week he walked to Bowling Green to the stock yard to buy old horses. He might buy as many as eight or ten at a time and with the tail of one tied to the bridle of the one behind it, he would walk home with a bunch of horses strung out behind him. When summer time arrived the heating stove was moved to the back porch out of the way. One day Glenn had been playing in the ash pan and had gotten his face and hands black with soot. When Daddy saw him he said, "You look like Pomp Hayes!" The name stuck.

Kenneth Roger: "Sid." When I was little, Sid Caesar was popular on the radio and always doing or saying something funny or crazy. Evidently I did something that reminded Daddy of Sid Caesar so the name Sid was hung on me. Probably no more than one hundred people outside of family know my real name is Kenneth. My wife and mother have always called me Kenneth.

Gary Steven: "Cicero Snowflake." Sounds like the work of a mad man doesn't it? We've no idea how he came up with that one for Steve. Eventually the snow flake was dropped and after that Cicero was shortened to Cissy.

Julia Louise: "Sook." Nobody knows why he called Momma Sook. If they were around strangers, he called her Julie. I wish I had asked her why, but Momma passed away long before I began writing this book.

After Daddy passed away, all the nicknames were pretty much dropped except for Sid and Buddy. I've actually had people say "Hey Kenneth" and I wouldn't even know who they were talking to. Duh! I have carried on the tradition without even realizing it. My daughter, Amy Lynn is B.B. for Baby Bear because she was so cute and huggable. Our oldest son Jeffrey Allen I sometimes call Jeffro Bodine and our youngest son Kevin I call Kev or Kevo. He lacked only a quarter ounce weighing ten pounds when he was born and I called him Heavy Kevy for a while until his mother stepped in and exercised her authority and I just decided to stop! Enough said.

One of a Kind
Julia Louise
1912- 1997

Julia Louise was born to Jim and Easter White. She was the fourth of five children belonging to Grandpa and Grandma White. Each of them had children by previous marriages. Grandpa had two children, Ollie and Ottie by his first wife who died. Grandma had a son, Willie Stanley by her first husband who also died.

There was Uncle Luther, Aunt Merttie, Aunt Sarah, Julia (Momma), and Aunt Gladys. It was a pretty tight knit family.

Grandpa was not much of a disciplinarian, but according to Momma he could do more by just scolding them than by whipping them. When Grandpa would scold them, it just broke their hearts. Momma said he wore an old felt hat and he would take off his hat and throw it down behind them and say "'Kays I Gad' I'm going to tear you up in a minute!" and it would scare them to death. She said he never whipped any of them even one time in their lives, but they thought someday he just might. Grandma on the other hand didn't put up with too much before she took a switch to you and she knew how to use one.

Grandpa was afraid of a thunder storm and when it would come up a cloud with thunder and lightning, Momma said he would run in the house, get under the feather tick with nothing sticking out but his feet and stay there till the storm had passed. So much for bravery huh!

Grandma on the other hand wasn't afraid of the Devil if she had met him in the middle of the big road, and if the right situation arose she had an extremely short fuse. She usually spoke her mind and if she was properly ticked off she could be down right ugly with you. Momma told us about a time when this fellow that Grandpa knew came riding up to the house about noon and Grandpa asked him to get off his horse and come in and eat dinner with them. The fellow declined, saying his wife would have dinner ready when he got home. I suppose Grandpa was lonesome for a man to talk to since Uncle Luther had already married and left home, so Grandpa asked him again, "Aw get down and eat with us," and again the man declined. Now Grandma didn't much like this fellow anyway because he had a tendency to brag and to lie. Grandpa started to ask him the third time to eat when Grandma stepped out the door and said, "Jim, get yourself a switch and whip that son of a bitch and make him eat." With that the fellow said "Well Jim, it's been nice talking to you, but I best be getting along. You all come to see us." Now that's the short fuse I was telling you about. Momma took her disposition from Grandpa and her determination and grit from Grandma evidently.

Lucky for us, Momma was never like that. She had more patience with her bunch of half wits than what seems humanly possible. She would occasionally switch us, but it never amounted to much, just sting for a minute and that was it. I can remember asking Momma to scratch my back where I couldn't reach and all she would do was rub it. Momma was a soft spoken, gentle, sweet lady, but there was one thing that absolutely sent her over the edge. If she saw a girl or woman wearing clothes that were too revealing, she would come off with her patented proposal for punishment. "Now, if I had a good keen switch I'd stripe those naked legs for her and she'd be glad to put some clothes on. The very idea of her running around half naked like that!" She could wear out a semi-load of switches today the way the girls dress. Maybe that was just a little bit of Grandma coming out in her! In our family the boys were taught to dress like gentleman and the girls like ladies, no exceptions period.

Calluses and Character
Phillip   Julia
1910-1961   1912-1997

People always said that Phillip Croslin was "a piece of work." He would grow into a man that stood six feet four inches tall, when the average man in those days was probably no more than five feet six inches tall. His hair was black as coal, and dark brown eyes, which gave credence to his claim that his mother was one fourth Cherokee Indian. He was always easy to find in a crowd. When he walked, he bobbed up and down and had the longest stride I ever saw. When they went to town, our Momma, who was five feet two, would almost have to run to keep up with him till she would say, "If you want me to walk with you, then you'll just have to slow down." There was always a goal in mind, and he meant to reach it! He thought nothing of walking eight or ten miles, or twenty if he didn't catch a ride with somebody. He could flat out cover some ground. He wore a leather cap year round, and a denim overall jacket in the winter time. We kids checked the pockets of his coat every day, because you just never knew when he might have peppermint sticks, or those little peanut butter logs, if he had been somewhere that had them for sale. He got a kick out of us doing that.

He was stern when he needed to be. Phillip never loaded you down with rules, but the ones he did have, you knew better than to break. He wouldn't tolerate one of his kids lying to him or to Momma, and you didn't back talk or sass either one of them. He worked hard and believed in doing a job right and with pride, and he taught us those same qualities.

The boys and girls both learned how to do things, such as how to plant a garden. Different seeds required different depths in the soil and different planting times. He didn't teach these things at the supper table. It was hands on, down in the dirt as they say these days. And the fact is, even though some of it was pretty hard work, it was fun! All of us were working together to accomplish a goal, and the goal was survival. Even a child five or six years old can drop a seed in the ground which is a very important task, so nobody was left out of an opportunity to do their part. Every year, for as far back as I can remember, we raised a garden, and very little of it ever went to waste. Daddy believed if there was more than we needed, there was some one that could use it, and he saw to it they got it. This was before the advent of chemical weed controls like people use today. The control over grass and weeds was maintained with a goose necked hoe, a mule and a plow. Several very important things happened here. First of all, you got rid of the weeds that sucked the moisture and nutrients from the garden plants. Secondly, there were no chemicals being absorbed into the plants, and then transferred into our bodies. The soil was kept loose for aeration, and that hoe handle made calluses on the hands. But maybe, even more importantly, those calluses turned into character. We never sat back and waited for someone else to feed us.

When my mother began public work as a nurse's aide, we grew the garden while she worked. Every afternoon when she got home from work, the girls had supper ready, and after eating, Momma would home can or preserve all the vegetables and fruit we had picked and made ready during the day. Imagine, an entire family working together like that. Do you suppose that would work today? Of course it would. Almost every home today has a back yard that is large enough for a small garden, that can be worked with a tiller, a hoe, and willing hands. You would be amazed at the amount of good wholesome food that can be grown in a twenty by twenty foot garden plot.

Momma did the same with the girls, in that she taught them how to cook, keep house, sew, preserve foodstuffs, and take care of their families they would have later.

This didn't just happen by us kids begging them to let us do things. We were simply told its time to do this or that, so let's get at it. That's where the calluses came from. We all became solid citizens and people to be trusted with your last dollar, or your life, or anything else for that matter. That's part of the character building Phillip and Julia imparted to us, and we're forever grateful they did!

The Great Orator
Phillip
1922

One of the greatest public speakers of all time was of course Abraham Lincoln. He was not only known as being wonderful in his delivery but the content of his speeches were historic as well. Many people have emulated Lincoln as a speaker and some have been very, very good at it. According to one of Daddy's old childhood friends Marshall Donoho, Phillip could flat out get it on in doing his rendition of Honest Abe. They both walked to school together, along with several other kids that lived near them. Someone had cut down a big chestnut tree on top of the embankment along Cemetery Road. This tree stump made a perfect podium for a speaker. As they would get close to this stump, Daddy would run ahead and already be standing on the stump as the other children came within ear shot. He would hook his thumbs in his overall galluses, rare back and at the top of his lungs deliver the Gettysburg Address without notes and probably without ever having read it more than twice. He always got a standing ovation since you couldn't have sat down in the middle of the road anyway. They would scream and cheer and Phillip would bow and they would go on their way to school.

There were other times Daddy would get in the spirit to preach on the way to school. He preached from the same stump where Abe had done some of his best work. All the kids loved hearing him preach, and even gave him a hearty amen when he made a particularly good point. It's a wonder God didn't send a lightning bolt and zap him off his stump but then again, maybe God thought Phillip had been zapped enough already in his short life.

Mr. Donoho said it used to just make him sick the way Phillip could make good grades and never crack open a book. They would have math bees that were like spelling bees. The teacher would send two or three kids to the black board at a time and give them problems to solve. Daddy never wrote down the problem. He would just write the answer on the board. He was automatic in winning these contests. Once he challenged the teacher and defeated her as well. It was all in fun but I would have been afraid of challenging the teacher since they taught all the other subjects as well. He would even whittle while classes were in session, but evidently he was good listener. I remember he could do math in his head before us kids could write the problem down on paper and I'm talking about some pretty fair sized columns of numbers. We kids were always amazed at this and he took pride in it as well.

He had the ability to hold people's attention when he was talking mainly because they never knew what he would say next. It might be too, that he never knew what he would say next either. For a man that didn't go beyond the eighth grade, he had a very good grasp of things. Phillip Croslin knew people, and was very much in tune with the natural order of things. He quite possibly was born at a time when he just almost missed being able to fit in with the ever changing world. It's like he was caught somewhere between the use of horses as a means of traveling short distances and automobiles as a way of seeing the entire country. The one place he did fit in was in our hearts and lives and I'm forever grateful.

Rocking and Rolling
Phillip
1923

After such a heart breaking start in life, you would think Daddy would have had a sour disposition or a huge chip on his shoulder. On the contrary, he was one of the most fun loving men I ever saw. He loved to laugh and would have jumped off the house if he thought someone would have gotten a kick out of it. He never worried about one thing in his whole life, except maybe when one of his brood was sick or hurt. Luckily, none of us ever had a life threatening injury as far as I know.

I was fortunate enough, after he died, to have known some of the people he grew up with and went to school with. Miss Willie May Kirby was two years older than Daddy, and would fill in as teacher in a little one room school when the regular teacher was sick. She told me that my daddy, Marshall Donoho, and another boy, whose name I can't remember, got in the old two-holer outhouse, got it rocking, and turned it over with the door facing the ground. They commenced to scream and holler like they were dying. All the smaller kids were crying, thinking the boys inside were dead or maimed. Miss Willie May and the rest of the kids tried to roll it over and get them out but the three boys would move to the side they were trying to lift, making it too heavy to move. They were moaning and groaning like they were dying. Finally, one of them laughed and Miss Willie May heard it. She then told one of the younger boys to fetch the Kerosene and a kitchen match from the school house, and they would just burn it off of them. One of three inside the toilet heard this and said, "Oh Hell! Let's get out of here!" and they rolled it right over without any outside help at all. Miss Willie May was in her sixties when she told me that story and she laughed till she cried and so did I. Come to think of it that was just the kind of thing I would have loved to have been in on myself. I guess the nut doesn't fall too far from the tree! I suppose that was why Miss Willie May was the substitute teacher. She was a pretty sharp cookie herself.

Dance with the One That Asked You
Julia Louise
1926

Normally my grandmother was a sweet old lady but if you got her stirred up she could bring some trouble on you. Momma recalled a time when they went to a dance at the Rocky Springs School House. Grandpa was an old time fiddle player and was always called on to play these dances along with Aunt Ollie on the banjo and Uncle Ottie on the guitar. They were quite accomplished musicians and had played together for years. The dance had just gotten underway, when this old man came up to where Momma, her sisters and Grandma was sitting and asked Momma if she'd like to dance. Momma politely turned the old man down so he returned to his seat and sat down. In a minute this handsome young fellow about Momma's age walked over and asked Momma to dance. She said she'd love to and they walked out on the dance floor. Just as soon as they started dancing here comes Grandma. She told Momma to go back to her seat and stay there. It was rude of her to turn one person down at a dance, and then instantly dance with someone else. It was embarrassing for Momma to be talked to like that in front of everyone. That was enough to take your taste for dancing I suppose. I'm not sure if Grandma was right or wrong in what she did, but there was a fifty-fifty chance she was right and a one hundred per cent chance she was the boss. In that day and time you had ground rules and they were not to be broken. If you by chance, choice, or oversight broke certain rules the punishment was severe and swift, end of story. My Momma had the utmost respect and love for her mother and always spoke highly of her.

Julia's First Love
Momma
1926

In nineteen sixty eight, I was working for the Coca Cola Bottling Company. I was calling on Walter Brown's country store at Bays Fork Kentucky. While filling the soft drink rack, this really cute girl came into the store with her father. I checked her out and our eyes met for a second before I loaded the empty soda bottles on a two wheeled dolly and went out to load them on the truck. In a minute, she told her daddy she would wait for him in the car and followed me outside where we struck up a conversation. We were not total strangers since we had gone to school together, but she was a couple of years younger than me. Well, it didn't take me long to ask her if she would like to go out and the best I remember it didn't take her long to accept the invitation. So the next Saturday night we went to the movies, and afterward were at the Dairy Dip having burgers and fries and of course cokes. We were having the usual first date small talk, when she said, "Did you know we were almost kinfolks?" I said, "How can you be almost kinfolks? You either are or you aren't kinfolks." She said, "Once upon a time your momma was married to my daddy!" I told her she was mistaken about that. She said "No, my daddy told me about it just today and momma knew about it too." I'm thinking this girl is a nut because I know my Momma has never been married before to anybody but my Daddy or I would have known about it! It was late when I got home and Momma was already in bed. The next morning when I wake up, this is the first thing on my mind, so I told Momma what she had said. Momma said, "Yes, I was married to him for a couple of months. It just didn't work out, so we had our marriage annulled."

You can't imagine and I can't tell you how I felt right at that moment. After the initial shock wore off, I got really mad that I was never told about it. Momma just said she thought everybody knew about it and it had been over forty years ago. So that was that! I never took that girl out any more, and it was never brought up again.

Expectations and Worry
Julia Louise
1929

What did the young girls dream about in the first quarter of the twentieth century in rural Kentucky? Did they dream of a handsome prince riding up on a beautiful prancing steed and taking them away to live in a crystal palace? With servants and hand maidens and all the luxuries known to man? Where every night was a Gala Ball with beautiful gowns and everyone danced the waltz? Maybe some did and maybe even our Momma did, but what they got was something so different, at times so nightmarishly different, as to be almost beyond belief. What they got all too often was a sharecropper husband and a house full of kids to worry over, worry with, and worry about. To work like a dog from sunup till sundown only to worry all night, had she done enough? Worry that something tragic might happen to one of her children, or her husband, or to herself. What if she died in her sleep like some people did, like her husband's mother did, and left all those children? What would become of them? These are the things I'm sure kept our Momma awake at night. Not princes, or galas or long beautiful gowns. Although even with all the hard work, hard times, and worry, I believe our Momma was happy. She had a husband who loved her, children who loved her, and a God that loved her and I believe she knew it and felt it.

Momma was fortunate not to have to help raise her brother and sisters since she was next to the baby. She was more fortunate than my sister Elizabeth had been. Lots of girls that were the oldest child that had helped care for several younger siblings got married at a very early age just to get away from that, only to wind up having a house full of children of their own. If this is depressing to read about, then just for a moment try to put yourself in their place, to feel the anguish they must have felt. Looking back, that's probably the reason Elizabeth waited eleven years before having a child of her own. It takes a long time to forget some things!

The only times I remember seeing a deep sadness in our Momma's eyes was when she lost our Daddy, our brother Robert, our sister Elizabeth, our brother Buddy, and her grandson Johnnie. They all died prematurely in life, some far less than the three score and ten written about in the Bible. There can be no worse hurt to a mother than to lose a child, no matter what their ages. Because they are a part of her, she brought them into the world and nothing can take their place when they are taken away. Our Momma knew more than her fair share of that kind of sadness!

There were, however, very few times you couldn't see the worry in Momma's eyes. That was just the way she was. If she didn't have an immediate situation to worry about, she just worried about what might happen. I know she never had a child that didn't give her cause to worry, some more than others, but we were all guilty, guilty as sin which many times was the exact reason she worried. I've often thought she was born to worry, but most likely most of her worries were born to her, all eleven of us, and I'll take my share of the blame and I'm sorry for that!

Fifty Cents a Day for Me and my Mule
Phillip and Julia
1930

The Great Depression hit poor country people just as hard as it did the rich. Yes we had a better opportunity to feed ourselves because we grew almost all our food but you can't grow shoes, clothes, and pay doctor bills. There just wasn't much cash money to be made and what there was came very hard. I remember my Daddy telling about working for wages plowing corn with a mule for fifty cents a day. That was twenty five cents for him, and twenty five cents for his mule. Had I been telling that story, I would have been inclined to say forty cents for me and ten cents for my mule. I think that would have sounded a little better. He also had to carry corn with him to feed the mule at noon time as well as feeding himself from what he brought from home. That was from can till can't, or daylight to dark for city folks. It takes a lot of gumption to do that day after day. He did that while at the same time taking care of his own crops. Momma did the milking and raised the garden. At the time they didn't have any children, but they did have one on the way. Elizabeth was born February 10th, 1931. Fifty cents a day sure isn't much income for two people to live on or should I say three counting the mule.

A man that owned the farm next to them had some land that he wanted cleared of trees, bushes and stumps. Daddy and Momma cleared that land for fifty cents a day, but the fellow did

37

furnish his own mules for pulling up stumps. I've wondered how many people today would work for the kind of wages they did in today's dollars. Daddy also picked up a little money for shoeing horses and mules on the side. He was always looking to make a little money as long as it was honest work. He trapped in the winter but hide prices went down when the economy went bust, since people could do without fur collared coats and other luxury items. Hard work was the only thing he and Momma knew and the goal wasn't necessarily to get ahead; to just stay even was a victory in itself and they always managed to do that.

A Whole Year, Shot
Phillip
1932

My Daddy was a tobacco farmer whether he liked it or not. He enjoyed working the soil, planting the seeds and watching them grow. He was a good farmer and loved what he did, but he didn't really enjoy growing tobacco and for good reason. Some things just take your taste away for doing a particular thing!

It must have been in the early thirties. He began in December to pile a plant bed. This was a plot of ground about twelve feet wide and a hundred or so feet long where brush was drug out of the woods and piled on top of some pretty good sized logs. These plant beds were burned at night along about the end of February after the wind had subsided to prevent fire getting out of control. The point in doing all this was the heat killed the weed seeds in the ground and the ashes kept the soil loose so the tender plants could be pulled up for transplanting without breaking them. As the brush caught the big logs on fire, you rolled the logs down the bed a little at a time. There was usually a fifteen to twenty minute period between rolling the logs, when some of the best stories you ever heard were told. In those days, men worked together on things like this, and they enjoyed the fellowship and the work. Tonight at one farm, the next night at someone else's place. The skyline at night would be lit up with an orange glow in just about any direction you looked. After the initial high towering flames were gone, the fire settled down to just keeping it going, and it usually was around midnight when it was finished.

The next day, the bed was raked and worked a little and the seeds were sown. Poles were laid along the sides and across the ends, stakes driven along side the poles and lastly, the cotton canvas was tacked down to the poles to create a mini greenhouse. Daddy always planted some radishes, beets, curly mustard, and lettuce inside the tobacco bed. This was for Wilt-Down Salad later on with hot bacon grease or ham grease drizzled over it. With pinto beans, corn bread hoecakes, and wilt down salad, we used to eat that and wonder what the poor folks were having. We didn't know it but the poor folks were having the exact same thing and we were the poor folks, but my, my, it was so good. Few things in this life are as delectable as wilt down salad!

A man counted on his tobacco here in Kentucky as a cash crop to pay for all the things a family needed that they couldn't make or grow themselves. There were no government support prices in those days. You got what the tobacco companies wanted to pay you for your crop and that was that. Take it or leave it was their motto. I think it was nineteen thirty one or two, Daddy hauled his tobacco crop to market, they weighed it in and it was a good, heavy crop that year. It was scheduled for a sale date, sold, and it didn't even bring enough to cover the floor expenses the warehouse charges for handling the sale and storage of your crop. Not to mention the expense for seeds, sprays and all the other things it takes to grow tobacco. And let's not forget the hard, back breaking, heavy work involved to grow a crop. It's always been said that raising tobacco is a thirteen month a year job. After they stole his tobacco, Daddy owed the warehouse three dollars for giving him the extreme honor and pleasure of being called a tobacco farmer. I'm sure he paid the three dollars, but he was a better man than I am I think.

What do you tell the person that runs the country store where you run a line of credit for a year, with the expectation of selling your tobacco crop and settling up your account? He has to eat and pay his bills just like you do. I don't know how Daddy was able to settle his debt, but if I had to guess, he probably sold a horse or a mule to get the money to pay up with.

The Big Hat Box
Phillip
1932

Years ago, this would have been in the 1930's, the carnival would come to Bowling Green every year and if you could scratch up enough money and a way to get there, you went. It was a happening as they say. My Daddy and my uncle Grover Guy went to the carnival every chance they got. That year like every year, they had attractions like the midway, the shooting gallery, and the usual stuff you would find at carnivals and county fairs today. But also back then they invariably had what everyone called the "Hoochy-Coochy" shows which have since been outlawed due to public outrage, because they had nude or semi-nude girls and Vaudeville type humor, even though you might see more skin at the Mall nowadays than they were showing then. While cruising around the carnival, they saw this huge, round, hat box looking thing with holes cut in the sides just above belt high. Men had their heads stuck in these holes and were straining one minute to pull their heads out and the next minute they were howling with laughter. Crazy huh!! Well that was just too much for Daddy and Uncle Grover to pass up. So they asked this fellow that had just had his head stuck in one of those holes what was in there that was so funny? He said, "Hell, boys, it don't cost but a dime to find out." That's all he would say. So, what else would two good ole boys like them do but to give it a whirl? They ease up to the carnie who was collecting the entrance fee, gave him their dimes and picked out a hole opposite each other. As soon as they stick their heads in the hole somebody throws a lever and they are caught like a cow in a milk parlor. The only way to get loose is to pull your head off. When all the holes had heads locked in them, out comes this woman that Daddy said must have weighed three hundred pounds and was about five feet tall. She climbed upon this huge turntable. This thing started turning real slow. This big old girl's butt was passing only a couple of inches from their noses. That would have been bad enough with clothes on, but she didn't have on any. She was naked as a jaybird. Oh, but it was hilarious watching the fellows on the other side as they tried to get away from it. But as they say, "What goes around comes around." Years later Daddy would get so tickled trying to describe the look on Uncle Grover's face just before she got to him. He said, "That woman surely had some kind of old stinking stuff she would put on her hind end just before the show because nobody could live long with their rear end smelling like that." He said he thought his ears were going to come off his head; he was pulling so hard to get away from that big old butt coming so close to his nose.

They decided not to ever tell that on each other, but time changes things. Heck, they couldn't wait to tell. They also highly recommended the hatbox attraction to some other fellows they ran into. Oh, the things we spend our money on.

Taking A Little Dip
Barbara
1944

Kentuckians have always had a tendency to like tobacco. They have for years and they still do according to the statistics. They love smoking it, chewing it, dipping it, and growing it. However, Phillip and Julia's three oldest girls took this to a whole new level in using tobacco in a way it was never intended.

Kentucky farmers in the spring time cleaned out the manure from the barn stalls, hallways, and sheds, then spread it onto the tobacco patch in place of store bought fertilizer. First of all it worked, secondly it was free, and thirdly it had to be removed anyway, so it was a win, win, win situation. Tobacco patches were usually in a low place in order to take advantage of the generally richer soil and the moisture is always better there than upland soil. In 1944, Daddy put the tobacco patch in a really low bowl shaped area with pretty steep sides. Another reason he did this is where he farmed it was more than gently rolling land. A goat could walk down into his tobacco patch but needed a ride to get out. So, you use what you have and hope for the best. From start to finish, growing tobacco is hard work, with the exception of carrying your money home after it's sold. That usually requires little effort.

The tobacco was really good that year and had already been topped when it come the mother of all rains. It was a chunk floater, and it filled the tobacco patch full of water almost completely covering the tops of the plants. Now if this wasn't bad enough, my three oldest sisters go take a look and decide why waste all this water? So they just go in swimming in daddy's tobacco patch. They had a grand old time kicking and thrashing around, chasing each other up and down each row without realizing the damage they were doing in breaking off leaves and riding the stalks over. They finally got out and went to the house, clothes soaked and muddy from head to toe. When Daddy came to the house that evening they were telling about all the fun they had in taking a little dip in the tobacco patch. He never said a word till the next morning after inspecting his crop. The water had receded significantly overnight, revealing all the damage they had done. Leaves were broken off and strewn everywhere. Like most all tobacco farmers, he depended on the money made from selling his crop to pay off the debt incurred in growing it and hopefully have enough left over to put food on the table, and buy clothes and shoes for the family and whatever else might come along. So to say he was a little upset is like saying Michael Jordan was only a fair basketball player. So he went to the house and called the girls outside and told them he was going to whip them for what they did to his tobacco. Elizabeth, the oldest took her thrashing first, then Jeanne, and then Barbara. Since Barbara had just witnessed the punishment rendered to her cohorts and saw nothing in it she couldn't do without, she decided she might play on his sympathy a bit. She commenced to hollering, "Oh Lord, Daddy! I can't breathe!" He said, "Well, honey, when I get finished whipping your hind end, you can go back to breathing."

No Way to Treat a Brother
Buddy and Billy
1946

Buddy and Billy were only thirteen months apart in age and like brothers can be, they had their differences at times. They usually got along quite well and played together like most kids will do. If you saw one, the other was never too far away. This story is true like all the others, it just doesn't seem quite right to anyone outside the family, that something like this could happen. There are two different versions to this story. One version was from Buddy's recollection and one from Billy's.

Buddy always said Billy got a brand new coat and he didn't and he felt like he should have gotten a new coat too. Whether that was true or not, it doesn't excuse the dirty deed that he did to poor old Bill. Billy always said that was just Buddy's excuse for being mean as a yellow dog. And who knows, Billy might have been styling and profiling his new threads and rubbing it in just a bit as well.

Years ago people built barns that had dual purposes. One end of the barn might have stalls for livestock with a floored loft. The other end might be tiered off for hanging tobacco to cure. The barn where this took place must have been built like that.

Buddy evidently in a fit of anger or just plain orneriness climbed up in the tiers and called for Billy. He shouted, "Hey Billy, come here! I've got something for you." Well here comes Billy on the run and without knowing, he comes in the barn and stopped directly underneath Buddy. It was just plain dumb luck. Buddy did a number on Billy and his new coat. Yep, he did the big number two right down the back of Billy's new overall jacket. Now Billy would normally have just torn into Buddy and they would have fought it out, but this was far too rotten to just beat up a fellow over. Billy lit out for the house and Buddy took off to the neighbors to hole up. Billy always said it was a good thing he couldn't find the rifle that day because he planned to just kill him and be done with it. Suffice it to say, when Daddy got home from work he gave Buddy a whipping he didn't soon forget. When I was talking to Billy while gathering information for this book, he got mad about it all over again, and that was sixty years ago. Come to think of it, I would still be mad about it too.

First Flyer in the Family
Robert
1947

Growing up in Kentucky in the late forties as sharecropper's children, your fun was just what you made it. There may have been store bought games around but we never had any of them. No computers or computer games existed, either. But what we did have was loads of imagination and we were always ready to use it in order to amuse ourselves. The girls always seemed to have a playhouse set up which usually consisted of a board laid across two stumps where they baked mud pies and mud cakes. There was never a shortage of mud at that time because several roads were still dirt roads. Their pots and pans were usually tin salmon and sardine cans. The only time boys came near these play houses was to wreck them or if you were too young to play with the bigger boys you were the baby in the girls' make believe family. The boys on the other hand had more macho things they had rather do and usually there was an element of danger involved. The junior members of those boys' clubs were mostly used as guinea pigs for some sort of experimental exercise which brings me to this story.

Whenever Daddy was doing work on the farm that was a one man operation, the boys usually had a day to play. They always followed him to the field if he was breaking ground in preparation for planting but they would play while he worked. One day while he was plowing, Buddy, Billy, and Robert went with him. Robert had finally escaped being the girl's play house baby. They were having a good time playing in the fence row that lined the edge of the field. They were riding over saplings. This is a game where you climb a small tree all the way to the top, get it swaying back and forth till it finally leans too far and bends all the way over and lets you down easy to the ground. The bigger you are, the bigger the sapling you can ride over--keeping in mind, when you jump off or let go, the sapling will fly back up really fast. Buddy and Billy hit upon the idea that if one boy can ride one over, then three boys in the same tree can ride over a really big sapling. So they look over their saplings till they find just the right one--a hickory that they decide will do the trick. Now remember, the Indians used hickory to make their bows for shooting arrows because they really had a lot of spring tension. So, all three of them start climbing this hickory sapling all the way to the top. When they get to the tip top, in unison they began to sway back and forth. It took a while to get it to the point of no return but it finally bent all the way over until Buddy and Billy's feet touched the ground. I'm not sure if they had it made up between them beforehand or if it was just a spur of the moment decision, but they both let go of the tree at the same time. Whoosh, back up it goes with Robert still in it and him and the tree parted company just past vertical. Out of the fence row flies Robert like a fat little bird. Luckily he lands unhurt in the soft dirt that had already been plowed at the edge of the field. Unluckily he lands right in front of the mules that Daddy is plowing with and scares them half to death. It's a good thing the plow didn't have wheels or they would have been in Butler County before he got them stopped. It's hard to run away with a turning plow socked as deep in the ground as a man can make it go by pushing down on the handles. Plus they were probably tired by this time.

As it turned out, Robert wasn't hurt nearly as bad as Buddy and Billy after Daddy got through with them. The next day Robert asked the girls if they needed any help in the play house. It's a wonder we all lived to be grownups.

Those Darn Flies
Tommy
1947

The state of Kentucky is a little like Texas in that lots of things are just naturally bigger, tougher, meaner, and taller than almost anywhere else in the country. Every other state in the union has mosquitoes but the ones here in Kentucky have longer drills that can almost reach the bone when they bite you. Our bigger ones are about the size of a small crow. Now that's just hearsay cause I've personally never seen one that big. The ants here are quite muscular fellows as well as being pretty large. One fellow in Butler County says he sat down under a tree while squirrel hunting and drifted off to sleep and when he woke up he was halfway to Louisville riding an ant. Now those are pretty hard to believe till you hear about Tommy's little incident.

Tommy was fortunate enough to have gotten a new sweater when he was about five years old. It was a pretty blue sweater, the kind of sweater most any kid in nineteen forty seven would love to have owned. There was only one problem. He wanted a red one. He cried about it and generally made quite a fuss over it until Daddy threatened to put a knot on his head. That satisfied him for a while, but Tommy could be down right persistent or stubborn about some things. This went on for a while until one day he was out by the wood pile playing. There, stuck up in the chop block was Daddy's double bit axe which was always razor sharp. We all knew never to touch it, but Tommy was on a mission. He pulled his pretty little blue sweater off and laid it on the chop block, then proceeded to take the axe and chop it to little pieces. After he was satisfied with his work, he went inside and told Momma to come and look. The darn flies had eaten his sweater up and when she went to get him another one would she please get a red one this time. He did get his red sweater and it matched his little red rear end perfectly.

Atta Boy Rob
Robert
1948

In nineteen forty eight, then and now, if you were a boy and lived in the country, you did two things for fun. There were other things you could do, but hunting and following the University of Kentucky Wildcats were at the top of the list of the most popular things for a boy to do. Hunting served two purposes with the first and most important was that it put meat on the table, and second it was just plain old good fun. Kentuckians always set great store in their hunting dogs. In fact, some of the finest hunting dog breeds have been developed right here in our beloved state. It was a source of pride to own a fine hunting dog. There were bird dogs, coon hounds, fox hounds, possum dogs, and beagles for rabbits. It just depended on the game you were pursuing.

My brothers Buddy and Billy managed to take this to another level. In Kentucky, it was a rite of passage to steal watermelons. Now don't get me wrong here, it is wrong to steal anything at all! It just shouldn't be done. But, swiping a watermelon falls at the lower end of the spectrum of serious crime when it comes to stealing. It wasn't encouraged by the parents, and anything beyond stealing a watermelon would have brought swift and painful punishment, as well as being marched right up, face to face, with the person you had offended, and making restitution as well as an apology to them!

A Mr. Nordrum lived on the adjoining farm to us and had a very fine watermelon patch. Not only was it a big patch of melons, it had some whopper sized melons in it. Now being a little bit on the mischievous side, and also not wanting to leave their younger brother Robert out of the fun, Buddy and Billy decided Robert would be their retriever. They would just pay a little visit to Mr. Nordrum's melon patch to see how he could do at retrieving melons. They took up a position in the fence row next to the patch, and after looking it over real good they spot the melon they wanted. Through a series of verbal commands and hand signals, they sent Robert on his hands and knees to the intended target. Poor old Robert really got in to the spirit of it all. He crept up until his nose was only inches from the melon before he went on point with one hand off the ground and one leg sticking straight out. "Atta boy Rob, fetch it," and with that he picked the melon off the vine and with it under one arm went back to the fence row. "What a good old boy you are," they told him as they patted him on the head. Then they dropped the melon, splitting it open, and the three of them ate it.

In their defense, they never damaged the vines nor took more than they could eat. This was the way it was done. By the time Daddy found out about their little scheme, I guess the Statute of Limitations had run out and so had the watermelons. He did however issue a stern warning, and that was enough to suspend their operations from that point on. Like I said, they were mischievous, but not really bad boys.

Weaning Time
Tommy
1948

    My brother Glenn was born in April of forty six. We lived at the Harry Brunson place on the Cemetery Road in the Motley community. Momma had weaned Glenn and we needed milk. Our cow was dry but Mr. Porter Meeks lived just across the field from us about a half mile away. He had a cow that he milked and she gave more milk than he and his wife could use. He would have most likely given us the milk but Daddy insisted he pay for it. Tommy remembers we paid a nickel per quart for the milk. So it was Tommy's job to walk over to Mr. Meeks' and get a quart of milk every morning for Glenn to drink and what Momma needed for cooking. Tommy was a strong sturdy little fellow and he liked going after the milk most of the time. It made him feel important to be walking around with a nickel in his pocket and to be entrusted with bringing home the bacon--or in this case, the milk. He's never been afraid of anything in his life and wasn't then. One particular morning he had walked over to get the milk. It was a pretty cold day in late winter, and on the way back home Tommy started getting cold. There was a fellow that lived between us and Mr. Meeks by the name of Benny Richey. He and Daddy were good friends and all the kids knew him very well. Tommy decided he would stop in at Mr. Ritchey's house and warm before going the rest of the way home. Mr. Richey relayed this story to Daddy the next time he saw him. He said, "I heard this knock on the front door and when I opened the door there stood Tommy. I said 'Come in this house, Tom, before you freeze to death. What are you doing out on such a cold day as this?' Tom says, 'Aw, I just been over to Mr. Porter's and got some milk for the baby, and I'll tell you one thing right now. If it doesn't hurry up and warm up some, there's gonna be a weaned little sum bitch at our house.'" Mr. Richey lost his breath laughing while trying to tell Daddy what Tommy had said. I don't know if Daddy whipped Tommy for the language he had used or not. I'd say he might have just let it slip his mind.

Oh, by the way, my brother Steve has still got the old single shot rifle Daddy bought from Benny Richey years and years ago. His initials HBR are carved in the stock.

Hard Headed
Tommy
1948

While living at Mrs. Georgia Willoughby's, the older kids were carrying in wood that Daddy had cut. There was a lot of it and they were not all that thrilled to be doing it to start with. To make matters worse Tommy was being a pest. Every time one of them would go to the wood pile, he was throwing hickory nuts at them. Now Tommy had a pretty good throwing arm for six years old and he was peppering them pretty good with those hickory nuts, then hiding behind a tree. They had asked him to stop several times but that was like saying siccum to a dog. He really stepped up his barrage on them. Finally Jeanne had enough of Tommy and his arsenal of nuts. There had been an old smokehouse that had burned and part of the chimney was still standing. She picked up a corner of a brick and put it in her pocket. When she got back to the wood pile, sure enough, Tommy let loose on her again. She pulled out the piece of brick and threw it at the tree he was hiding behind just to scare him or so she said. She missed the tree but he stuck his head out just in time for the brick to hit him in the top of his little bean head. Down he went, cold as a wedge. "God, I've killed him!" said Jeanne as she yelled for help. So they picked Tommy up and carried him to the house. He started to come around by the time they got him to the house. Momma sat him down and was washing the wound out with kerosene. Everybody was crowded around them looking at the wound. Elizabeth said, "Oh Lord, I can see his brains." She really couldn't, but she was very excited and scared. When Tommy heard that, out he went again. It turned out to only be a scalp wound, but I guess he felt like he had been scalped. He still carries that scar around on his head to this day. It blends in well with all the others he has picked up over the years. How our Momma kept her sanity while raising her brood I'll never know.

Kenneth Roger
Sid
1949-

     I was the tenth of eleven children.
December 12th, 1949, the night I was born, it
came the mother of all rains. It was what we call
in Kentucky a chunk floater or a frog strangler.
Momma told Daddy it was time to go get Mrs.
Della Moseley, who was a midwife and had
delivered several of my brothers and sisters. She
was batting a thousand because Momma had
never lost a child in childbirth. I'm not sure how
Daddy got hold of my brother in law Kenneth
Mitchell to take him to get her. We lived above
the Cold Springs bluff on Drakes Creek at the
Paul Allen Hunt place. When Kenneth and
Elizabeth got to our dirt road, he was afraid they
would get stuck in the mud, so they walked the
rest of the way in to the house. Daddy and
Kenneth then left walking back to his car. This
was during the Rural Electrification project in
Warren County. The R.E.A. had hauled utility
poles out, and dropped them where they were
going to be erected. By this time it had gotten
dark and Daddy never could see very well after
dark. The heavy rain had backed up water
behind one of these poles lying on the ground.
When Daddy got to that pole, he hung his foot
on it and tripped, falling head first into this pool
of water which was about a foot deep. He was
not a happy camper to say the least! They finally
got Mrs. Della back to our house in time to
deliver me. I was born about a half hour later.
The house we lived in was old and had a leaky

roof. Daddy told me once they had to move the bed Momma was in several times to keep me and Momma from drowning. What a way to come into this world! My sister Elizabeth cooked breakfast that next morning and Daddy said the biscuits were floating like steamboats from the rain leaking in. Obviously he was exaggerating a lot, but still that was a time when most folks would have sat down and cried, but not Phillip. Hell, he had just had a brand new baby boy and Julia and the baby were both doing fine, and he was ready to go out in the world and kick its butt. It never dawned on him I guess, that he already had enough baby boys and girls. Oh, and by the way, he named me after my brother in law Kenneth. I guess that was his payment for taking him to get Mrs. Della. I never heard what he gave her for her services. Doctor G. H. Freeman came the day after I was born to check Momma and me. He said we were fine except my right leg was slightly longer than the left but probably wouldn't bother me too much. He was right, it never has, but the right leg is one and a half inches longer than the left. I began to experience back pain at about forty years old due to the curvature of the lower spine caused by the leg imbalance. I grew to be six foot four inches tall. Of all the kids, that was the closest any of us came to having a birth defect of any kind. Thank God.

Feed Sack Dresses and Hand Me Downs
Everyone
1930s-1950s

Throughout the early years of Philip and Julia's family, we did what most all families did. We barely scraped by, and we did it only by the slightest of margins. We did it by working hard and doing without. Oh, we had food to eat and clothes on our back, but most of the food we grew ourselves and the clothes were handed down from one to another until they were just too far gone to use. Back in those days Momma made the girls' dresses from chicken feed sacks that her sister Sarah would save for her. The companies that sold chicken feed realized the way to sell their feed was to give those that bought it a little something extra. So they had their supplier for sacks use material that had a pretty print on their cloth sacks. Women would take these sacks and make dresses out of them to wear. They could actually be very pretty dresses depending upon the skill level of the seamstress. She also made shirts for the boys from them. They were durable as well and might go through three or four hand downs before they were worn out. A stranger might have thought there were several sets of twins at school because most people used the same patterns and prints. There was no shame or embarrassment associated with these clothes because they were clean and neat.

It never ceases to amaze me today when I see people buy a new pair of jeans with holes already in the knees and legs. Fifty years ago it would have been so embarrassing to go to school with holes in your pants yet today it's fashionable. Go figure!

I wonder how many shoes today are actually worn out before buying new ones. There was a time when you wore them until a hole came in the sole, then you took them to a shoe repair shop and had them resoled and continued to wear them till the tops were completely worn out. I've worn shoes with the sole worn down so thin, I could step on a dime and tell you whether it was on heads or tails! I was visiting my sister recently and saw a box in her garage with about five pair of shoes all lined up nice and neat. What struck me as unusual was they all looked like new. When I asked her about it, she said they were just her "yard shoes." Wow, and to think she only has two feet! I guess we've come a long way from feed sack dresses and hand me downs!

The Little Man in Black
Tommy
1950

Whenever Momma got dinner just about ready, she always knew what part of the farm Daddy was working on, so a few quick calculations told her when to send one of the kids to tell him to come to dinner. One particular day, it was drizzling rain when it was getting time to go get Daddy, so she gave Tommy an old black raincoat to wear and sent him after Pop. The tail of it was dragging the ground but that didn't matter, he was still dry. He walked down an old logging road through the woods to the field where Daddy was plowing corn with a mule. Just before he got to the field, he saw Daddy coming up, riding Old Roudy. Now Roudy was a gentle mule only because he was lazy as a dog. He would have thrown you if it just hadn't been too much effort. Daddy felt perfectly at ease riding him side-saddle. He'd just jump on and let his legs dangle off one side. It had rained him out, so he had unhitched from the rastus plow and left it at the end of the last row. So here he came with his back turned to the side toward Tommy who had stepped behind a tree. He was going to scare Daddy as he passed. When Tommy stepped out from behind the tree, Old Roudy went ballistic. With that old black raincoat on, Tommy must have looked like a Martian to Old Roudy. One big jump and Pop was airborne. When he hit the ground he landed flat of his back, knocking the wind out of him. By the time he got his breath and started getting up, Tommy and Roudy were both gone--Roudy to the barn and Tommy to the house. A little later Daddy came in and Momma asked him, "Phillip, how in the world did you get mud all over your back?" He said, "That damn fool mule just threw me tree top high. I don't know what got into him." Momma never mentioned that Tommy had told her what happened. That wasn't the only time Momma covered for one of us either!

Chariots and Ire
Buddy and Billy
1950

We were living at Mrs. Georgia Willoughby's in the Claypool community in nineteen fifty. While most farmers had begun using tractors by this time, Daddy still worked mules and horses. We had corn down in the creek bottom. Since Daddy didn't drive or own a car he would catch a ride with Lucian Westbrooks on the milk truck and ride to town to take care of any business he may have had. On this particular day, before leaving the house he informed Buddy and Billy they were to plow corn until he got back from town. It was early July and very hot. He instructed them to walk the mules back to the barn at dinner time and to feed and water them before they went to the house to eat. They used riding cultivators back in those days to plow row crops. So the boys set out for the creek bottom right after breakfast and Daddy walked out to the main road to catch the milk truck to town. When he got back home he was almost to the house when he heard a lot of hollering and whooping and cultivators clanging and banging. The noise was coming from the road that leads down to the bottom land and the cornfield. Daddy's first thought was the mules were running off with the boys and they might be killed. He lit out running toward the cornfield to try and head them off. Just as he got to a little bend in the road he was nearly over ran by two boys that were standing up on these cultivators chariot racing. Each one had a switch off a tree, urging the mules onward as fast as they could run. It was the very first chariot race ever held in Warren County, Kentucky. However, it was not an event that was sanctioned by the supreme commander in our family and the punishment was severe and immediate. When Daddy got to the barn, the boys had already removed the harnesses and were watering the mules. He had walked slowly in order to cool off from the run, the heat, and his ire. When the teams were properly taken care of, so were the boys. He used their very own switches from the great race on them.

If Daddy had asked them why they did it, they would probably have told him they had learned about chariot racing in the Bible and were only trying to get a real understanding of it. Of how the Egyptian soldiers may have felt as they tried to run down the departing Israelites before they got to the Red Sea. Yeah right! Now these boys were good at self preservation and nothing was off limits when it came to avoiding the ire of their sire.

Breaking Out of the Pen
Sid
1952

By the winter of fifty one, we had moved to
the northeastern edge of Warren County in the
Claypool community. The house was off the
main road back through the woods to a clearing
of about five acres. That winter is still talked
about by old folks as being the worst they ever
remember. Everything was covered with ice, and
Daddy said the tree limbs breaking from the
weight was constantly waking us up at night. We
had a wood heater which stayed red hot trying to
keep us from freezing to death. There was no
electricity or running water in the house. The
only running water we had was when one of us
ran to the spring to get it. My baby bed was
pulled pretty close to the stove to keep me warm.
I was about thirteen or fourteen months old by
now and was standing up holding on to the side
of my baby bed, jumping up and down having a
good time when the side broke out and tossed
me head first into the heater. Momma had just
stepped into the kitchen to check on her meal
she was cooking. My brother Glenn was about
four and a half years old at the time and thanks
to him he was able to pull me away from the
stove even before Momma could run in there. He
must have been standing really close to me or it
may have been all over for me. I still have a scar
on my forehead about the size of a baseball
which really shows up after I start losing my tan
in the winter. People that have known me all my
life still ask me what's happened to my head.

People I don't know sometimes ask me about it and I tell them I got it breaking out of the pen. That's all I tell them and they usually don't ask me anything else. They think I broke out of the big house.

My baby brother Steve was born while we lived there at the Mrs. Georgia Willoughby place. I remember when he was born I had to stay outside all afternoon. After a while I started wanting to go inside and see my Momma. The only way they could satisfy me was to give me a biscuit broken open with a little dab of sugar sprinkled on it. It took about three of those before I was allowed back in the house. By then I had lost my position as the baby in the family. That took a while for me to get over too. It was never lonely at the bottom.

Crank or Bust
Barbara
1952

My sister Barbara graduated from Alvaton High School in fifty one and she was the class Valedictorian that year. (I was the dropoutatorian in sixty seven.) Not bad for a sharecropper's daughter huh? She then enrolled in the Bowling Green Business School which had a nine month program. It was an eight in the morning till four in the afternoon class schedule, Monday through Friday. She got up every morning, milked two cows, got dressed and walked a half mile to the Cemetery Road to catch a ride with Mrs. Mary Roddy into Bowling Green to school. Mrs. Mary wasn't the most punctual person in the world and Barbara was late for class two mornings the first week. The teacher asked her to stay after class on Friday because he wanted to talk to her. He asked her why she was late so often. After Barbara told him her situation he said, "Well I guess that will be all right." We all need a little understanding at times and it was very good of him to overlook her tardiness since it was beyond her control.
She got a job after graduating from business school at the National Advertising Company in Bowling Green. They sold billboard ads. There was a nice young man that came to work there by the name of Jack Keyser who would eventually become her husband and they would be married for nearly fifty seven years until his death in 2009.

Shanty Hollow Lake in northwest Warren County was a very scenic little spot. It was just the kind of place in 1952 where a romance could blossom with a picnic on the lake. Barbara and Jack took a picnic lunch to the lake, rented a small motor boat and found a lovely little spot up the lake for a shoreline lunch. After lunch when it was time to head back to the dock, the boat motor wouldn't start. Jack began cranking on this motor and just wore himself completely out until, out of breath, he dropped down on the boat seat. Now Barbara was a very beautiful, petite country girl that milked cows as well as other farm chores, and even though she was not very big, she was strong for her size. So in order to help out she said, "Jack, let me try my hand at that." So they traded places in the boat and Barbara began to crank the motor. After a few pulls Jack felt bad about her cranking on it and decided to swap positions again. He stood up behind Barbara just as her hand slipped off the crank rope handle and she hit him dead center in the crotch with her hand. He fell like he'd been pole axed. Oh, the embarrassments, the pain they both must have felt because remember, this was 1952 and things were much different then from now. Eventually the motor did start and they returned to the dock somewhat the worse for wear.

For the next couple of weeks Jack was the high tenor in the church choir which probably had folks wondering how you go from a rich baritone to high tenor in only one week. He had just graduated from the "Barbara Croslin Marine

Technical School for Ad Salesmen." They both recovered in time.

Lying Wounded
Tommy
1952

Country boys in Kentucky seem to have an affinity for guns. Not for terroristic purposes like you might hear about today, but for hunting wild game such as deer, turkey, rabbits, squirrels, and quail. They grow up around them, are taught to use them safely and effectively. We were no different in that we used them to put meat on the table. With a family our size it sure did come in handy. There is nothing better than a big platter of young squirrel fried to a golden brown, and hot biscuits, and squirrel gravy. My Momma could have put the chicken king out of business if she had marketed this.

All the boys in our family liked to hunt and Tommy and Buddy were almost like Indians when it came to hunting. They seldom ever came home empty handed when they went hunting. In fifty two, Tommy decided to go squirrel hunting, so he took Daddy's single shot .22 and headed down on the bluff overlooking Bay's Fork Creek, which wound around Mrs. Georgia Willoughby's place where we lived at the time. There were lots of hickory nut trees there which are the favorite food for squirrels. One simply looks for cuttings on the ground which tells you the squirrels are feeding off a certain tree and you wait quietly till they start coming into it to eat. With a .22 you can sometimes get as many as you need without ever moving from one spot. Tommy was watching for squirrels while leaning on the rifle with the end of the barrel under his arm which is a no-no under any circumstances and he knew it. He did it without thinking which is almost always the cause for hunting accidents. The gun stock had been setting on a root and slipped off causing the rifle to go off and Tommy was shot under the arm. He ran home and told Momma that someone had shot him from across the creek. He remembers it only bled a few drops--the bullet missed the shoulder bone and you could feel the slug just under the skin on top of his shoulder. Daddy was working for the R.E.A. at the time and wasn't home. So Momma sent Wanda and Glenn to our neighbor Dewey Cassady's house to ask if he would come and take him to the hospital. Now our Momma was no forensic specialist but she was no dummy either and she could tell from the angle of the wound that no one had shot him from across the creek. When she asked him what really happened he knew the jig was up and he confessed that he had shot himself by accident. When they got him to town they took him to the doctor's office where the doctor examined the wound, then just simply split the skin on top of the bullet and removed it.

In an about two weeks he went back and retrieved the rifle where he had left it. He lost his taste for hunting for a few days but he learned a valuable lesson. In the state of Kentucky, there are numerous gun safety classes taught every year, and still several people each year are killed or injured in hunting accidents. It happens because people just don't pay attention to safety, even when they know better. Tommy was a prime example and he would be the first to tell you that! Our poor Momma never knew what to expect next in our family.

Power to the People
Julia
1953

A new age was dawning in Kentucky's rural communities around the late forties and early fifties. That's when the Rural Electrification Association or R.E.A. came to Warren County. It lit up the rural homes with electric lights instead of kerosene lamps and lanterns. This brought about a drastically different lifestyle for country people, my people, who had seen the light when they visited Bowling Green, and they wanted it as well in their homes. It was wonderful being able to see well all over a room and not just if the kerosene lamp was right next to you. It had to have been hard on the eyes, straining to read the Bible or other books as well as sewing and the like. Not only the light was terrific, but appliances to make life easier were being used more and more. Some people even had electric powered washing machines and to top that, they had little portable water heaters you plugged in and dropped into the water in the washing machine to heat the water. They were only about eight inches long and six inches wide with holes through it to let the water into the heating coils. I can tell you from experience those little heaters would give you a curly perm if you stuck your finger in the water while that little bugger was plugged in. It was slow to heat the water, but would heat you up pronto. This was such a nice improvement to everybody that had electricity in their home, but unfortunately Phillip and Julia lived in a sharecropper's house that was way back off the road and not feasible for the landowner to have electricity put in. Mrs. Georgia Willoughby was a really fine old lady, and she lived right on the main road and I'm not sure if she even had power in her own house at the time, and she owned the land where we lived. We had a washing machine, but it was a gasoline powered model. You had to use a flexible steel pipe to run the exhaust out through a window if you used it inside in the winter. In the summer time it sat on the back porch and Momma did the washing there. It was still a vast improvement over the old washboard she had used before the washing machine, except for one thing. Momma could never start the thing when she got ready to wash our clothes. It had a foot crank that you stomped to crank it. Daddy was always in the field working not long after sunup before Momma got ready to wash. When she was ready to start her washing, she would commence to stomp that crank trying to start the motor and keep at it till she wore herself completely out. She'd rest a minute or two and fly in on it again to no avail. Finally she would give up and start using the washboard to do the laundry. By the time Daddy came to the house for dinner she was fit to be tied and all through dinner she'd harp on that washing machine. Now my Daddy was a bright fellow and he knew a fire would eventually burn itself out if it ran out of fuel, so he just listened. After he finished dinner, he would go to the washing machine, give it one stomp and it would take off like Lindberg. He'd just ease on out of the house like he'd stolen something and go back to his own rat killing. This made her even more frustrated, but by the time he came back in the late afternoon she was fine and the clothes line would be hanging full of nice, freshly washed clothes, and all was right with the world, or at least until the next wash day!

The Girl I Hardly Knew
Jeanne
1955

In the nineteen thirties, forties and fifties, there was a widespread disease called Tuberculosis or T.B. as it was most commonly called. Many people carried the T.B. germ, but the body usually fought it off. When a person became run down due to other illnesses or poor diet, the T.B. germ would attack and override the body's immune system. If left untreated, it was a deadly disease that most usually attacked the lungs but could affect several organs. The disease was highly contagious and throughout the country, there were Sanitariums built for treatment and isolation.

When my sister Jeanne was sixteen years old, she developed T.B. and was committed to the Riverside, Kentucky Sanitarium for treatment. The sanitarium was about twenty miles from our home in northwest Warren County. My Daddy and Momma went to visit her every other week and took her whatever she might need while she was there. I remember going with them to see her and not being allowed to go in with them. That was hard for a child to understand, that he couldn't even see his own sister.

The one thing I remember most about it was when she would come to the second floor, raise the window and talk to us, her baby brothers and sister. She always had on pajamas and her hair was jet black like Daddy's and I

thought she was the prettiest girl I ever saw, and on top of that she would always talk and joke with us. She never failed to throw us packs of Juicy Fruit gum out the window. I'm sure it was part of the things they had just carried in to her so we could share something together with her. The best we can remember, Jeanne was in the sanitarium there about two and a half years, and when she came out, she was cured.
She was never again a very strong person physically, but she had the quickest mind you ever saw. She was funny, witty, and could be downright ornery when she wanted to be. I was talking to her one day and she stopped and said to me, "Oh Sid, do you know how to keep a moron in suspense?" I said, "No, I guess not." She said, "Well, I'll tell you tomorrow maybe." It took a minute for her little joke to set in, but I grudgingly decided maybe she did know after all!

She and I once went fishing on Barren River, which was just across the road from our house. It was a high, steep bluff and we had to pick our way down carefully to the river. Jeanne had always fished with a cane pole we had cut and dried for making fishing poles. I had bought a couple of cheap fishing rods and reels and Jeanne wanted to borrow one of them. She was about fifty feet down the river from where I was fishing, and the current had washed her hook into a log and hung it up. I looked around just in time to see her backing up the bank with the rod tip pointed straight at her hook trying to pull it loose. Her fishing line sounded like someone winding a banjo string tighter. Before I could tell her that was a no-no, her hook pulled loose and here comes this hook and sinker out of the water like a torpedo. The hook missed her, but the sinker, a big old chunk of lead shaped like a dinner bell didn't, hitting her right smack dab in the middle of the forehead. Down she went like she'd been shot, flat of her back and just about knocked out. By the time I got to her she had started to groan and began trying to get up. I asked her if she was all right and she muttered, "I think so, and when I get my feet back under me, I'm taking my hind end to the house." I said, "Don't leave just yet; I want you to get my hook un-hung for me because I'm afraid to try it myself after what I just saw." She talked to me pretty rough for a little bit but finally saw the humor. She turned and started up the bluff while I gathered our poles. It didn't take me long to catch up for she was moving real slow. We had several laughs about that little fishing trip over the years. Jeanne and I were always pals, and just enjoyed laughing and talking about old times together.

Memory Trips
Sid

If I try real hard and think back on it enough, lots of things come to me that I haven't thought about in years. Things like the smells of a warm kitchen, and homemade sausage and eggs cooking, and hot biscuits coming out of the oven.

I can also remember the sounds of sleepy kids filing into the warm kitchen, to finish getting dressed near the wood stove. Looking back, the kitchen was always the center point of our house. I mean this is where the action took place. Big, important decisions relating to the welfare of our family were made there. It's where we ate three meals together, not just on Sunday, but everyday of the world; we shared the events of the day around that old table. It's where I stood up at the corner of the table next to Momma and ate for two or three years, and thought nothing about it, totally satisfied with my lot in life. It's where after supper, when the table was cleared and the dishes washed, it was turned into a study hall and discussion forum with topics ranging from world events to what happened at Curtis Weaver's store that day. It's where I had the honor of reporting how Mr. Willie Brummit had jumped down off the store's front step that morning, and the jolt had ignited a big old box of Diamond brand kitchen matches he was carrying in his hip pocket. Man, did he ever do a dance trying to put that fire out. Instead of dropping and rolling, Mr. Willie was rocking and rolling. I can still see the smoke and flames shooting out of his hip pocket as he ran across the store porch. I felt just like Dan Rather reporting the evening news when I relayed that little tidbit that evening at supper time!

I remember when Saturday afternoon rolled around we all got excited about going to Dee Howell's little country store, if Daddy could scratch up a dollar or two. We weren't going there to shop; we were going to watch the "rasslin" as everybody called it, and to have a big RC Cola and a Moon Pie. The rasslin from the Hippodrome in Nashville was on a little television set at Dee's store, on the topmost shelf. The store was about twenty feet wide and thirty feet long, and it would be standing room only on Saturday night. A chiropractor could have done very well indeed every Monday morning just by realigning people's necks after a Dee Howell rasslin match. Just about all the men had a kid sitting on his shoulders so he could see the television set, for everybody loved the T.V. in those days. Had we only known what a conversation killer and evening waster they would become, the family unity and harmony may have been saved. The only time I ever heard my Momma talk dirty was years later in her own home while she was watching the wrestling on T.V. The good guy had been taking a terrible butt whoopin for about fifteen minutes and Momma was mad enough to die, when Pop, Slap, Boom, her boy made a comeback and was pouring it on the dirty old man he was wrestling. Momma was so torn up watching this, she said, "I hope you beat the living hell out of that

S.O.B." Only she said the real deal. Then it hit her! She had just talked dirty and had done it in front of her kids. Even though I was already married, she still couldn't believe she had done that. She said, "If that's the best I can do, I just won't watch it anymore." As far as I know, she never watched "rasslin" again!

Now, whoever planned professional wrestling was a marketing genius for they knew how to pick the bad guys. This was right after World War II and the American people didn't need much of an excuse to hate a German or a Japanese, and that was usually who the bad guys were. This one old villain manager of two German wrestlers, Saul Wiendropf, was hated even more than Hitler in nineteen fifty three. If his boys were getting whooped, he would sneak into the ring and crack a good guy over the noggin with a cane which of course was against the rules and everybody knew it. Heck fire, even the preachers in the area hated him, and those two Germans. Had Saul Wiendropf ever passed through Claypool or Settle, Kentucky, he had better have made sure he didn't have to stop for anything. He would have been beaten worse than a chicken thief and strung up immediately. Anti-dirty rassler sentiment ran high at Claypool, and Settle, Kentucky in the early fifties!

Going Big Time
Glenn
1953

With the advent of gasoline powered tractors, farming went through a real transformation in this country. From steam powered stationary equipment such as threshing machines and hay balers, to steam powered tractors that were huge, slow and dangerous. Then along came the more modern tractors that were faster, better built, and safer. The days of using horses and mules to do farm work were coming to a close. Daddy tried to hold on to the things he knew and understood best but even he could see the writing on the wall concerning farming practices. He knew it was time to change.

In the spring of fifty three, Daddy decided we needed to upgrade our farming operations. He heard about a fellow that had an F-20 Farmall tractor for sale, so he went to look at the tractor and find out what the man wanted for it. I don't know what the man was asking for the tractor but it couldn't have been much. The problem was, Daddy didn't have much money but he did want the tractor. According to my brother Tommy, Daddy wound up trading this man a fine little spotted pony we had to the tractor. I would guess this tractor was pretty well worn out when we got it, but Daddy was really fired up to finally own one even if he couldn't drive it. It didn't have a muffler, and the radiator leaked like a sieve, along with all the other assorted problems. I barely remember the tractor but I do remember you started it on gasoline and after the engine warmed up you switched it over to kerosene. (See, you thought "dual fuels" was a brand new concept.) It also had steel rear wheels with big steel cleats and rubber tires on the front. The first day they used it they were doing the spring plowing down in the creek bottom. I guess they had a two bottom plow, which instantly doubled the output over the team plow he had always used. That evening at supper Daddy was so proud of his trade, and talked about all the work they had turned out with his new acquisition and how he would increase the acreage next year since we now owned a tractor. Glenn was only about five years old at the time and wanting to back Daddy up he added, "Yeah and it only took two mules and a wagon to haul water to it." The next day Glenn got to stay at the house and help carry wash water for Momma. Some things are better left unsaid!

Crack Shot
Jeanne
1953

In Kentucky now days there are quite a few young girls that have taken up the sport of hunting and I think that's fine. Its great exercise and good therapy to be in the outdoors and it gives dads and daughters something to do together they both can enjoy. It sure beats hanging out at the mall all day! They also fish and that's great too. I think a thirteen year old girl now holds the state record for muskie. You go girl! Things are very different now than sixty years ago. Not many girls hunted then and only a few more fished.

When my sister Elizabeth was born Daddy was fine with that and was very proud of his little girl. She was pretty as could be and they were always buddies. When the next baby came he was proud of his second daughter as well, but deep down he had wanted a boy this time. So without even realizing it, he'd started treating her like she was a boy and that was just fine with Jeanne. She tagged along with him when he went squirrel hunting and rabbit hunting. She learned to shoot a .22 rifle and by the time she was a teenager she was one fine shot. I remember sitting with her on the front steps and watching her pick blue tailed lizards off an old dead tree in our front yard which was at least one hundred and fifty feet away. The bark on the tree had started to come off in places and it made a perfect lizard hotel. It wasn't long till every room was vacant. She also had very little trouble killing a mess of squirrels with that rifle. Many years later when it was only her and my mother living together and they would get burned out on the same foods day after day, she would take that same old .22 rifle down behind the house to a little patch of woods and in no time she was back with a squirrel or two and they would have squirrel, squirrel gravy and hot biscuits for supper.

I doubt they can beat that at the White House in Washington D.C. It would be funny to have one of those state dinners with foreign dignitaries visiting and announce to the Grand Doo Dadd from where you ma call it, "We're having Squirrel, Squirrel Gravy, and hot biscuits for dinner." With food like that they might not want to leave!

Sudden Illness Syndrome
Glenn
1954

I suppose since the beginning of time or whenever they started having schools, there have been certain people that absolutely loved going to school. They had a real thirst for knowledge of any kind. They soaked it up like a sponge, and I suppose that's good if you happened to be one of those people. You've all seen the type, where every afternoon they took every book they had home with them from school. Now some only did it for show while others actually studied every one of them. I fit neither of those groups and my scholastic standing reflected that especially in anything beyond the sixth grade. Now Glenn on the other hand was a pretty good student and liked school most of the time. But, bless his heart, (if you're a Christian and you're going to talk about somebody, that's how you should start off) every once in a while Glenn would come down with what I generally refer to as "Sudden Illness Syndrome". A very strange illness this S.I.S... It's like one minute you're just feeling wonderful, so full of energy and life, and the next minute you are just about lifeless and the weird thing about it is there are no outward symptoms such as fever, rash, vomiting, or the trots as we always called it. The first notice that you're about to be struck down with it usually comes from such things as Daddy saying, "I believe I'll go fishing a little while today," or "Julia, I guess we better go to town today and take care of some business." Its only known cure has to do with the school bus running in the morning without you on it, and there is no other way to get to school.

Legend has it that Glenn was struck down with S.I.S. one morning even after he and the rest of our brothers and sisters had left the house to walk the half mile to the bus stop. After just a little ways from the house it hit him full force and he said he reckoned he had better turn for home before it got him plumb down. Even though the others advised him against trying it alone, he told them not to worry about him--he believed he could make it. And by taking it slow and steady he finally got back to the house but it was close. Momma was busy in the house and Daddy was probably behind the barn digging fishing worms when she heard the faintest sound at the door. She couldn't recognize the sound as it seemed more like a scratch than anything else. When she heard it the second time, it was even weaker sounding, so she decided to go see what it was. The Lord was watching over poor old Glenn that morning for by the time he got to the house he was so far gone all he could do was scratch on the screen door. Momma promptly brought him into the house and started checking him out. It didn't take her long to diagnose his problem. Yup it was S.I.S. Thankfully, he pulled through and by the time Daddy had a salmon can full of fishing worms dug he was feeling well enough to go to the creek with him. Bless his heart!

Party Poopers
All of us
1954

In 1954 we lived at the Mrs. Georgia Willoughby place in the Claypool community in the northeastern edge of Warren County. The community hub was Mr. Curtis Weaver's store. It was where most everyone went for short term supplies such as milk and bread, radio batteries, cokes, candy bars and once a week the ice man came and you could buy block ice in twenty five and fifty pound blocks. Daddy usually hauled it home with a mule and ground slide. He took a couple of quilts to wrap it in, to keep it from melting on the way home if it was hot weather. A twenty five pound block would last a week if the ice box door wasn't opened unnecessarily. Needless to say, we didn't stand with the door opened and stare into it. That would have gotten you swatted on the behind. Ice was a precious commodity in those days before electric refrigerators.

Once in a while Mr. Curtis would host a community gathering at the store and he would serve some kind of refreshments; usually it would be home made ice cream. Everybody enjoyed these gatherings since you didn't see each other all that often. It was an opportunity for the men to talk crops, mules, horses, and swap funny stories. The ladies especially enjoyed it because they saw each other even less than the men. Us kids ripped and ran playing all sorts of games and just had a fine time playing together. There was never any trouble between us. What a simple time it was to live back then. It was almost perfect peace and harmony in those days.

One particular time Mr. Curtis started spreading the word on Monday that they would be having a get together the following Saturday night. After everyone had finished doing up their night work as they called it (milking the cows, feeding all the livestock, putting the chickens up) and eating an early supper they made their way to the store. The Grand Old Opry was usually on for those that liked it and most everybody did in those days. Television hadn't found its way to Claypool yet. Usually after about an hour and a half it was time for refreshments and this time they served chocolate bars broken up into little squares. It wasn't terribly expensive because a candy bar only cost a nickel in those days. They placed these little squares in a bowl and passed it around. We were taught to not be greedy as was most everyone else there with the exception of Amos and Jr. Babe who were two older bachelors that lived in Allen County. When the bowl got to them they dug in with both hands like a steam shovel dipping coal. This really ticked Mr. Curtis's daughter off that they would be so hoggish. So she eased around and told everyone but Amos and Jr. Babe to not take any chocolate pieces when it was passed around again. She then grabbed all the laxatives off the store shelf, broke them into little squares and passed them around. Everyone said no thank you; they had had enough chocolate for one night except Amos and Jr. Babe. When she got to them, they broke out the steam shovel dippers again and scarfed down the treats she offered. Everyone continued to have a great time for an hour or so. All of a sudden, Amos and Jr. Babe started to get fidgety, twisting and turning in their seats with a pained expression on their faces. Both men were crossing and uncrossing their legs, re-adjusting their caps and before too long they gently left their seats and eased out the front door.

The county line where Allen and Warren join is only about a quarter mile from the store. It was reported by a reliable source that they tracked Amos and Jr. Babe all the way into Allen County that night on a black top road. They had just caught some little something that was going around.

This Ought to be Good
Buddy
1954

Music has always been an important part of most Kentuckians' lives. Most families had at least one person that had at least some musical talent. They might play piano at church or guitar at home for their own entertainment, and some of them have been very successful in the music business over the years. My Grandpa White was an old time fiddler that Momma remembers playing every night after supper. He was a very accomplished musician according to her, and they loved hearing him play the old reels and waltzes. She said it sounded like his fiddle was talking to them when he played. That sounds to me like a most peaceful way to spend an evening with your family in Kentucky.

When Buddy was about fourteen years old, he got interested in music. We always listened to the Grand Old Opry on an old battery powered radio every Saturday night. Gibb Cassady, a family friend who lived nearby, was a blind man that played guitar and he wasn't much older than Buddy. He taught Buddy his first chords and after that he was hooked on country music for life. Buddy and our sister Jeanne started singing together and were pretty good for just a couple of kids with no real training in music. They even got to sing on one of the local radio stations and had quite a following and were eventually regulars on the show.

A friend of mine, Glenn Richmond, told me this story many years later while we were both serving on jury duty. The little country store at Green Hill in Warren Country from time to time would have something going on of a Saturday night to bring in business and to promote fellowship in the community. In nineteen fifty four there wasn't a lot going on in Bowling Green for people to do, so they really turned out for these get-togethers. Glenn remembers going over to the store that night, where someone had backed a pickup truck right up to the store front. Up walks this kid with an old plug of a guitar and climbs up in the bed of this truck. There was no introduction, no sound system, no nothing but this kid and his guitar. Glenn remembers thinking, "Well this ought to be good. I should have stayed home tonight." Glenn had been to the Opry before, and had seen live country music shows by Opry members at the local high school gyms and he knew what good music was. Now here he was at Green Hill store where a kid was about to sing. He told me when Buddy started singing there was about ten people standing around listening. But in ten minutes time the store was empty and everyone was outside listening to this kid. He said he sang for about an hour, one song right after the other and he was spellbound as was everybody else. Glenn said he would have stayed all night if he had sung that long. He had never heard anything like it before or since.

Buddy was one of those people who were good at whatever he wanted to do. He could listen to a car motor and tell you exactly what was wrong with it and then fix it. He was one of the best automatic transmission mechanics anywhere around this area.

He was loaded with talent but short on ambition, which was a shame as good as he was, but I suppose he was happy doing what he did. I really believe he could have been a star with the right kind of help because he had everything it took talent wise as well as being downright handsome too. Musically he was my hero!

One Tough Man
Phillip
1954

In Kentucky there were many times if a person got sick or hurt they just had to tough it out and that in itself could be dangerous. Transportation being what it was for a long time; you didn't hop in the car and run to the doctor every time you got a runny nose or a hangnail. Many times money figured into the equation, and lots of folks like us didn't even own a car to begin with which added to the problem. But as the saying goes, "Tough times make tough people."

We were living at Mrs. Georgia Willoughby's place at Claypool in fifty four when Daddy came down with an abscessed tooth. His jaw was swollen terribly and he couldn't eat or sleep for the throbbing pain. All he could do was walk the floor and hold a sock full of hot table salt on his jaw. That was an old remedy that didn't work, but everybody tried it if they got to hurting bad enough. After suffering for three days and nights he had had enough and decided something had to give. So he set off walking to Bowling Green to find a dentist to pull the tooth. There were a few country doctors around the county then but no country dentists. He had walked about six miles to Hardcastle, which was about half way to town and came to Forrest Jones's house. Mr. Forrest had just finished eating dinner and was sitting under a shade tree resting before going back to work. He was a friend of Daddy's and he hollered and told Daddy to come up and cool a bit. When Daddy sat down, Mr. Forrest asked, "Phillip, where are you headed on such a hot day?" Daddy told him about the toothache he'd been having and that he was going to get it pulled somewhere or somehow today. Mr. Forrest asked which tooth it was, and Daddy showed him the jaw tooth that was killing him. Mr. Forrest said, "Why, Phillip, that tooth is too far gone to save. I can pull that tooth and won't charge you a thing." Daddy said, "Well bring 'er outta thar! It's hurt me all it's going to." So Mr. Forrest got his fencing pliers, leaned Daddy back against a tree and pulled the tooth. No Novocain, no charge, no nothing. Daddy washed his mouth out with kerosene, sat there for a few minutes, got up and walked back home. My entire head hurts just thinking about that to this day. He could stand some pain and that's a fact! Mr. Forrest himself told me that story years later and he said, "That Phillip Croslin was the toughest man I ever saw!"

Years before that, Daddy was chopping some kindling for the cook stove. He was holding the small stick of wood with one hand and the axe with the other when the axe slipped and the razor sharp blade came down right across his left pointer finger where the finger meets the hand. It hit the knuckle, disjointed it and only a little bit of tissue in the palm was holding the finger on. He folded the finger over into his palm, went in the house and wrapped a towel around it, walked down to the nearest neighbor that had a car and had him take him to the doctor. When he arrived at the doctor's office the towel had soaked clear through with blood. They saw him immediately and as the doctor started examining his finger, he told the doctor to just finish taking the finger off and he'd be on his way. Luckily the doctor was more stubborn than Daddy and also a pretty salty old boy. He said, "Hell fire, man, I can take it off when I can't do anything else!" He repaired the damaged finger and was able to save it. He had about eighty percent use of it after that. Mr. Forrest was right about Daddy; he was one tough man.

Nothing Left But the Chimneys
All of Us
1954

Along about the end of fifty four, my grandma got really sick. She was in her early eighties, and lived with my Aunt Sarah and Uncle Logan about five miles from us at the time. Momma got word she was maybe about to die so Daddy hitched up the team and wagon, loaded everybody in and we went to see Grandma. We stayed all day and night while Momma looked after Grandma. She improved overnight and that afternoon we headed home. When we broke out of the woods into the clearing all that was left of our house was the chimney and a little smoke from a pile of embers. We lost everything but the clothes we had on and what was in the barn. People from all around came bringing clothes, furniture, pots, pans, and the like. We were right back on our feet and running again. My Momma's half sister, Aunt Ollie Guy and Uncle Herschel lived only about a mile away so we went to their house and stayed till Daddy could locate another house to rent. Uncle Hershel was just about one of my favorite people and I loved being around him. So did all the rest of us. I don't remember how long it took to find a house but when we did, it was clear across the county near White Stone Quarry. A Mr. W. D. Fizer owned a farm there and had beef cattle. Daddy made a trade to take care of his cattle and tobacco, in exchange for some money, half the tobacco crop, and a house rent free. Now this house was in really good shape, with electricity and even indoor plumbing. Wow, a bathroom in the house! Momma also had her first electric stove for cooking. She was so proud of it. It was the first time Momma and Daddy had ever had such nice things. We were certainly more comfortable there but we weren't any happier as a family because we didn't measure happiness in material things. I don't think any of us ever have.

About four trades and four houses later, we got hammered again. Another home burned. This time we were at home when it started. Momma was always a light sleeper, and about two o'clock in the morning, she awoke to the smell of smoke. She started yelling, "The house is on fire!" And it was on fire in every room I think. The electric wiring had somehow shorted out and it had started the fire. I remember all the running and hollering in getting everybody out. This house had two front doors. The wooden steps on one of them had gotten in bad shape and Daddy had torn them down and was going to replace them. In the meantime, to keep anyone from accidentally walking out that door and falling, he had nailed the screen door shut. When Momma sounded the alarm, my brother Robert grabbed me up and with me under his arm, he ran against that screen door like a pro football running back taking it completely out. That entire screen door flew at least twenty feet out into the yard. I'm glad it was summer time when we would leave the wooden door open to let in a breeze. I may have been hurt bad if he had hit that wooden door with me right out front like a pointy headed battering ram. We were all out of the house in probably thirty seconds or less, and then Momma started calling us each by name to make sure nobody had been left inside.

Under every bed in the house, in the closet floors, and anywhere else Momma could find a place to store it, were hundreds of home canned fruits and vegetables we had grown, picked, peeled and canned. Hundreds of woman, kid and man-hours had been spent in putting that stuff up. That was what poor folks lived on in the winter. That and meat we had put up. We stood in the gravel road in front of the house and watched it burn. There were no fire departments in the county at that time, and unless one had been next door it wouldn't have been able to save the house. I can still hear in my mind those glass fruit jars exploding from the heat--muffled pops like popcorn in the microwave sounds now. Momma cried because she knew what each one of those little muffled pops meant. Each one meant one less dish of food that winter that would have to be found somewhere else. That's a lot easier to say than do!

We never knew for sure what caused the electrical short, but in no more than twenty minutes the house was falling in. This time we only got out with our underwear and gowns. Even the keys to the car burned up. It was setting in the driveway beside the house. We were able to push it far enough away to save it.

Once again, the neighbors God bless em, all pitched in with whatever they could spare. We were still afloat, which just goes to show, share croppers are just like a weed that's been stomped and ground under a boot heel into the dirt, only to spring back to life with a little time and rainfall. You can't keep a sharecropper down. People in Kentucky have always had that kind of spirit and determination about them!

Make Room for the Baby
Steve
1955

Steve was born September 28th. 1953, and for a long time I didn't much like him. In fact, I didn't like him at all. He had taken my position as the baby in the house. Now that came with some real perks such as being carried a lot if the walking was rough, and sitting in Momma's lap when we went somewhere in the car. (That was long before seat belts and child restraint seats were ever thought about.) All sorts of things went to the baby in the family, especially the attention and praise for doing even the simplest things. But the best thing was getting to sleep with Momma and Daddy till you were at least three years old or you were bumped out by a new baby. Such was the case when Steve came along and I was bumped into sleeping with Glenn and Tommy. It takes a while to recover from such a traumatic experience as that but I managed somehow.

Things went very well indeed for Steve in his lofty position and it didn't take him long to realize the power he wielded just by being the baby. But then even the Pharaoh got busted. Steve was about two years old when his troubles began. He had learned he could hold his baby bottle nipple in his teeth and by rolling his head from side to side he could really make that bottle fly from one side to the other. Remember, this was a heavy glass bottle which might even be considered a blunt instrument. He was practicing this maneuver when Daddy turned over in the bed just in time to get hit just above the eye with that baby bottle. It split his eye brow enough to bleed considerably. You never heard such a commotion as took place with Daddy cussing and stomping through the house looking for something that would stop bleeding. I couldn't help but derive a good bit of satisfaction from the event taking place, and if Daddy had asked, I would have told him he had never had such a sorry thing as that happen while I was the king, or rather when I was the baby. Daddy had a high tolerance level for the baby, so it wasn't long before Steve was back in his good graces, but then some people just can't handle success. Such was the case with Steve, when just a few nights later the unthinkable happened. It was late in the night when all hell broke loose again. I was awakened to "Damn it Julia, this kid is eating me up!" It seems that Daddy had rolled over onto Steve's bottle, and when he couldn't pull it out from under Daddy's arm, he resorted to the only tactic he knew. He just leaned over and tried to chew Daddy's ear off. He bit him clear through the ear. He bled profusely and that was the final straw. Daddy put his hand on Steve's head and pushed him as far down under the cover as he could reach, then took his foot and pushed him the rest of the way out off the foot of the bed. King Steve was dethroned and his reign was over.

I don't remember who got bumped to make room for Steve in our bed but most likely it was Tommy. Maybe that's where he got the

nick name "Pore Boy." Glenn and I invoked a
rule of "No Bottles Allowed in Bed."

One Fine Little Machine
All of Us
1955

Our Daddy was born at a time when most everybody traveled by horse and wagon or buggy and that's what he identified with more than automobiles. He completely understood horses and mules and was gifted at training them to work. In fact he broke teams for people all over the county. They brought them to him in the fall of the year, usually when they were about two years old. He would spend the winter training them to pull whatever he hitched them to and to follow his commands. By spring time they were pretty much broke to work. He used them to raise a crop with that year, and the owners would pick them up in the fall. They would, as we used to say, be dead broke by then and gentle as kittens. He would charge so much per head for the training, plus he got the use of them for that year. Automobiles were another story altogether. Although he was usually a pretty progressive thinker, he refused to learn to drive one. Owning one was one thing but driving one was another matter. He just flat wasn't interested in learning to drive. So, if he needed to go to town on business, he would just catch a ride on the milk truck that morning when they stopped to pick up our milk. He would take care of his business while the truck was being unloaded. The truck driver had to wait till the cans were emptied and washed before reloading the empties on the truck to return to each farmer. He would meet the milk truck at a prearranged location that afternoon and ride right to our house. There was never any charge for this. This worked out alright if it was just one person that needed to go, but was somewhat of a hardship if the entire family wanted to go anywhere. So when Buddy was old enough to drive, Daddy bought some old used cars to haul us around in. We seldom ever all went to town at the same time since it was so much trouble for Daddy to obtain a parade permit.

I remember a 1946 Ford coupe we had when I was about five years old. Daddy bought it from a used car dealer in Bowling Green for a hundred dollars. That seems like a pittance today, but in 1955 that was a fair amount of money to a man that probably never had more than three hundred dollars at one time in his entire life. It was such a pretty little car--light blue with red fender skirts, and we felt like we had hit the mega bucks lottery. Boy, were we uptown in that little old car. When we all went somewhere in it, every piece of glass in it had a kid's face stuck to it looking out.

Now here's the picture I'll try to paint. This was a two door coupe that would uncomfortably seat five small people. My three oldest sisters had married by this time, so counting Momma and Daddy there were ten people to ride in this car. The seating arrangements had to be worked out like an airliner, before we took our first ride in it. My oldest brother Buddy was the chauffer and boy was he cool with those dime store sun shades on. My youngest sister Wanda rode in the middle front, then Momma with Steve in her lap. She was a heavy woman and just couldn't get in the back seat. Left side rear was Daddy's spot so he was in easy reach of whoever was driving, in case they went faster than his thirty five miles per hour speed limit. Glenn sat next to Daddy and Billy was in the center with Tommy in his lap. Robert held down the right side. I always will believe I had the best seat in the entire arrangement. I had the area behind the back seat in the rear window lying down crosswise. I could see better than all of them in that I could look where we were going or where we had been. Had we run into something, I would have just hit all those heads in front of me and stopped. I would have fought a man over my spot. Plus, had we gone somewhere more often, I would never have lost my summer tan with all that sunshine coming through the rear window on me.

Daddy, with Buddy driving, brought the little car home on Friday and announced that we were going to visit my grandmother on Saturday. Grandma lived with momma's sister Sarah and Uncle Logan. My grandpa had died a few years before. I know Daddy wanted to do something nice for Momma by taking her to see her mother, but what he really wanted to do was show off his little Ford. We lit out early Saturday morning right after milking the cows and eating breakfast. We were off and running on our big trip. It was so exciting to actually be going somewhere in our own car. Every little bit, Daddy would say, "Ain't this one fine running little machine?" It didn't bother him that every slight dip in the road we came to, the rear bumper would drag the pavement from the heavy load that little machine was hauling. But we were still moving and that's what mattered. We had been liberated and it was sweet, oh so sweet! It was about eighteen miles or so to Grandma's and by the time we got there we were all sick of hearing Daddy talk about what a fine little machine he owned. Also we were a bit tired of hearing about what a fine fellow that car dealer was for selling him a machine of this quality for only a hundred dollars.

Upon our eventual arrival at Grandma's, running at thirty-five mph, we all needed some relief from hearing about a fine little machine and wonderfully sweet used car dealers. I suppose Daddy was just blinded by success. We began to pile out of that little old car, and it probably looked like school had let out. Front seat first, then the back. We had to help Billy and Tommy both out because their legs had gone to sleep shortly after we left home. When all of us but Daddy was out, he stood up, bent at the waist getting ready to step past the folded over front seat back, when the floor board just gave way from rust and his right foot went all the way to the ground. He turned the air blue a cussing. I had heard some pretty fair cussing before, but he brought forth what I believe to be the best I had ever heard. He normally didn't cuss very often, and one might have thought he would be out of practice, but with that many kids he probably was kept in a steady supply of reasons to cuss because we were constantly into something. We thought one of us might have to crawl under the car and take his shoe off in order to extract his foot from the hole in the floorboard. But he finally calmed down enough to get it out. It didn't worry us too much because a skinned shin bone will heal in just a few days if left alone and doctored with a little coal oil.

We had a really nice time visiting Grandma, Aunt Sarah, and Uncle Logan. While writing this, I had a thought that if the brakes had failed on the way home Daddy could have just put his foot down through that hole and let it drag to help slow us down. I'm glad I never thought of it then, because I may have been just stupid enough to mention it to him. Thank God for watching over me even then. The hole in the floorboard did, however, let in a little cool fresh air on the way home which came in handy because one of us had stepped in some chicken crap that day.

It's amazing how one's perception of a fellow human being can change in such a short time. Daddy went from just about loving that car dealer to hating his guts in about a milli-second. I never had thought about all the different ways you could hurt a man till then and Daddy described all of them on the way home. He had a plan but Momma's cooler head prevailed that time. By the time we got back home she had talked Daddy out of killing a used car salesman.

What's in a Name?
Kenneth
1956

The people here in the Commonwealth of Kentucky have always set great store in names. We are a people that love to pay tribute to folks that hold a prominent place in our hearts, by naming our children in honor of them. It's probably safe to say that half the people here have some sort of a nick name as well. My Daddy nicknamed almost every one of us. Our Momma told us that before Glenn Ray was born, Daddy already had a name as well as a nickname picked out for him. I'll bet that's a new one for you. She said Daddy wanted to name Glenn, Lucien Monroe and call him Mon. Lucien Westbrooks was a friend of Daddy's that owned and operated the milk truck that hauled our milk. Daddy was also a Bill Monroe fan so that's how he came by the name. Momma had no problem with Lucien Westbrooks or Bill Monroe, but none of her children was going to be called Mon and she knew the only way to prevent that from happening, was to name him something else, and do it quick! Daddy even named a mule he once owned Abraham in honor of Lincoln. Heck, lots of folks here in Kentucky even named their cars, trucks, and tractors after people they knew or that were famous. A really powerful tractor was likely to be called Hercules or Samson. We actually had a car once that had a stiff clutch which gave it a tendency to leap or lurch ahead when the clutch was let out. The name for this car came easy since one of Daddy and Momma's favorite people was my Aunt Lena White, which was usually pronounced Leaner, so we called the car Leaping Leaner in honor of her. She loved it when we told her we had named the car after her but also added that we shouldn't expect her to do any leaping since she was getting along in years.

My most favorite name of all time in our family belonged to a dog. We always had dogs as far back as I can remember and they had powerful, rich names like Ol Bullett, or Ol Jack or Ol Suzie. We lovingly added the Ol to their names even when they were pups. It just showed them we cared about them and respected them I suppose.

There was a fellow back in the fifties by the name of Marvin Whitley that knew our Daddy very well and knew he loved dogs. Mr. Whitley had moved from the Hardcastle community to Ky. Highway 101 which was a very busy road. He had a big yellow cur dog that he was afraid would get run over and killed on 101, so he offered to give it to Daddy for he knew he would have a good home with children to play with. Daddy told him he would love to have the dog and would come after him the first chance he got. So one morning a few days later my brother Buddy (Hugh Wright Croslin) took Daddy to get the dog. Mr. Whitley didn't know they were coming so he fed the dog that morning which is a mistake if he's not used to riding in a car. They visited a little while before loading the dog in the trunk and heading home. Buddy was a huge country music fan and picked and sang every chance he got. Someone had given him a big box of country music song books and they were in the trunk of the car. When they got home with the dog and opened the trunk of the car, a terrible smell hit them right in the face. Our dog had gotten sick and had thrown up right in the face of a smiling country music singer whose face was on the top front page of those song books. Daddy said, "Well, I can see that dog thinks about as much of that S. O. B. as I do." Daddy claimed he threw up a meat skin that still had the government stamp on it. I would never have even tried to verify that, but Daddy always paid attention to detail. So from that day forward our dog was called Ol Puke. We kept Ol Puke for years and he was a constant companion. I could have sicced Ol Puke onto a grizzly bear and I'd put my money on Ol Puke winning the fight. I guess with a name like "Ol Puke" you had to be one tough hombre and he was tougher than a fifty cent steak.

Wow and Goodbye
Sid
1956

I began my school days at Alvaton High School in nineteen fifty six. I went through the first grade and half of the second grade there before we moved. This time we moved into the Rich Pond school district, where I finished the second grade and half of the third grade before we moved again. Guess what, we were back at Alvaton again. We moved a couple more times but still stayed in the Alvaton school district. All this time I was a good student making mostly A's with a B thrown in there once in a while. I can't say I ever really liked school all that much but I did the work. The best part of my time at Alvaton was when I became sweet on my first girl friend. God she was cute as could be. She had a twin sister just as cute but there was just something about this little girl that really got to me. Their mother would do their hair in those finger curls and as she walked, her curls would spring up and down. She was neat as a pin and had dimples when she smiled. After more than fifty years I can still picture her just the way she was in the third grade, wearing a navy blue jumper with a white blouse neatly pressed and black and white saddle oxfords with white lace topped socks. I had it bad huh! What a girl. The only problem was I was too shy to tell her. You haven't heard the last of her either.

By this time Daddy had been forced to retire from farming due to a heart condition. He had been diagnosed with a leaking heart valve several years earlier and the problem had continued to worsen and at that time there was no fix for it. His doctor told him he had to slow down and take it easier if he wanted to live. We had been living on a dairy farm, milking over a hundred head of cows twice daily, as well as putting up silage and hay for the cattle. It was just too much for him, and my brothers weren't all that happy in the dairy business. So after moving to just a rented house we were never again farmers. The house we moved into needed fixing up and we asked the owner about it. We planned to stay there a long time. He said, "Phillip, you do what ever you want to the house and you can stay just as long as you like." So, we began painting, hanging new wallpaper, fixing up and cleaning up. We spent countless hours and several dollars in the restoration of that old place. It looked great! Nice as could be! Then the owner came by one day after we had been there about a year and said, "Phillip I'm getting married and I need my house. You have got to be out in sixty days." Just our luck... So off we go again, this time to Richardsville, which was clear on the other side of the county. I liked going to school there. I made lots of friends and straight A's.

Snakes and Birds and Dirty Words
Phillip
1950s

I suppose the natural fear of a snake comes from the Bible in Genesis where Eve is tempted by the serpent to eat of the forbidden fruit. God punished the serpent by making him crawl on his belly in the dust and Man would bruise his head and he would bruise the heel of Man. Phillip wasn't afraid of a snake of any kind, at least the ones you find in this part of Kentucky and believe me there are some pretty bad snakes around here. I've seen him pick up a snake, twirl it around his head and pop its head off just like cracking a whip. He felt it was his duty to pop a snake's head off rather than to just bruise it. Once when we were having a Sunday picnic at Martinsville Ford on Barren River, a huge snake of some sort came crawling across the gravel bar we were playing on right toward us. Once we spotted it we started screaming "SNAKE" and here came Daddy on the run. That big old snake coiled up ready to strike when Daddy ran up to it.   He yelled, "You kids get back out of the way and I'll take care of him!" He stood there until the snake started to crawl again and when it was stretched out crawling Daddy grabbed it by the tail, picked it up and swung it around his head a couple of times and popped the snake's head off. That was fine except the snake's head hit me right up side the head. I then proceeded to have three fits and a bad spell. I just knew I was probably going to die in the next minute or two. Luckily I wasn't hurt but you can bet your rear end that from then on I knew how far "get back" meant. They washed the snake blood off my head in the river and checked for puncture wounds but didn't find any thank goodness!

I remember my sister Elizabeth started to open a closet door once and a snake's tail fell out in her face. She took off through the house screaming like a banshee and didn't stop till she was way out in the yard. Daddy went in the house and opened the closet door and when he came out of the house he had a copper head snake about three feet long minus its head. He had popped that sucker's head off right in the house. I guess he knew it was too dangerous to try taking it outside. After throwing the snake over the fence in the pasture, he went back inside and got the head and buried it where we couldn't find it. Like any of us would want to.
I don't think there was but one thing my Daddy was afraid of in this whole world and that was a baby bird. I know that sounds ludicrous after the snake tales but he was terrified of a baby bird that didn't even have feathers on it yet. You could have ran him out of the country with one or until he got to a gun which ever came first. I asked him once why he was so afraid of a baby bird and he said the only explanation he had for it was when he was a small child when he would visit his Daddy for a few days while his Daddy was working, his step-mother would put him in a room and lay a big old feather duster in the doorway. He was terrified of that duster and he would go to the far corner of the room and cower

there till she removed it before Grandpa came home. That has always struck me as just about the most sorry thing a person could do by scaring a child that badly. That was probably only one of the reasons why he never had any use for his step-mother and as far as I'm concerned that would have been enough. I truly doubt that Grandpa ever knew she did that. Surely he didn't know about it.

Jacob Talley was a good friend of Daddy's and they swapped work with one another. That was a common practice in those days in order to get time sensitive work done in a hurry as well as a good way to fellowship with one another. We were there helping Jacob set tobacco one year and had quit for dinner. After dinner the men all went out on the porch to rest and smoke before starting back to work. Daddy had set down on the porch floor and leaned back against a porch post to rest. Jacob's youngest son Clarence (whom everybody called Fuzzy) had found a baby bird that had fallen from the nest. Now Fuzzy and everybody else knew Daddy was afraid of a baby bird and he should have known better, but he pitched that dead baby bird in Daddy's lap. You never saw such a fit as he threw. He was running and cussing wide open. When he finally did get stopped the fear was instantly replaced with anger and here he came after Fuzzy. Now Fuzzy knew his business had better lay rolling so he ran like a haint. Daddy told him later if he ever did that again he would knock his head off and he wasn't smiling when he said it either. We all knew he meant every word of it.

I guess everybody is afraid of something, even something as harmless as a baby bird! It's another example of our human frailties!

For a Good Breath of Air
Steve
1957

When Steve was born, he seemed like a normal healthy baby boy. It wasn't long before Momma and Daddy realized he had a problem. There was something wrong with his breathing. They took Steve to see Dr. Freeman, a country doctor here in Warren County that everyone knew and trusted completely. Today when you say something about a country doctor some people might think they were not very good. And I suppose some weren't, but some modern city doctors today aren't considered very good either. But Doctor Freeman was thought of as being among the very best to be found in the city or country. He examined Steve and gave Momma and Daddy the bad news. Steve had chronic asthma and he had it bad. Not all that much was known about asthma at that time and there were no really good forms of treatment. But with what he knew and had to treat it with, Dr. Freeman kept Steve alive, but it was touch and go for a long time.

I remember sharing a bed with Steve and he would just stop breathing and the next instant he would sit straight up in bed without ever waking up. You could tell him to lie down and he would but in a few seconds he would pop right back up. The asthma sort of leveled off for a while but then it started getting worse. Along about this time, Doctor Freeman realized it was time for a change. There had been some advances in the treatment of asthma, and a new doctor had come to Bowling Green who Doctor Freeman had met and was much impressed with. He said, "Phillip, I want you to take this little man to see Doctor Keith Coverdale. He's just opened a practice here and I believe him to be a very fine doctor and your best chance to save this child's life. I'll set you up an appointment with him immediately." It scared us all when he said it's your best chance to save this boy's life.

Now I've told you that the only thing our Daddy ever worried about was when one of us was hurt or sick. Well this really shook him up. He walked the floor day and night until their appointment with Dr. Coverdale. I remember him as being a very gentle caring man.

He began treating Steve and he saw him just about every week it seemed for about two years. There were lots of shots involved in his treatment and it didn't take Steve long to conclude that anyone with a white uniform on was to be avoided if any way possible. If we were in the car and he saw a milk man wearing a white uniform he went all to pieces. But under Dr. Coverdale's care, he began to improve. The doctor told Momma and Daddy that he believed in time, Steve would grow out of most of the asthma problems he had been having and sure enough he did. He grew up to be just about the stoutest built one of the bunch.

Bare Knuckle Champ
Wanda
1957

We were living at the Porter Meeks place in fifty seven. It was hot summer time and not much to do, so I was sitting on the corner of the concrete back porch busting hickory nuts with a claw hammer. I soon tired of that and was just setting there deep in thought when I began tapping on the porch with the hammer. I was lost in my own little world and the next thing I knew, I was really swinging that hammer hard which was chipping the concrete. My sister Jeanne came flying out the door, screaming at me to give her that hammer. Without thinking, I threw the hammer down on the concrete and ran. It bounced up and hit her in the shin bone and down she went like she had been shot by a cannon. She was taking on pretty bad and talking about Florida of all places. Something about a sunny beach I think. Anyways, here comes Wanda out the door like a raging bull, and since I was all out of hammers I took off for somewhere else. She chased me all the way to the end of the road where she finally overtook me. I'd seen some mad folks in my time but not like she was that day. She had killing on her mind. She commenced to whipping on me, putting knots on my head faster than I could rub them, and dragging me back to the house to see about Jeanne. By the time we got back to the house, Jeanne was feeling some better and for some reason she wasn't even all that mad at me. I guess she could see Wanda had already dealt out punishment enough on me.

I really did feel bad about hitting Jeanne with a claw hammer, but to try to get a little sympathy I sat in the yard and pretended I had some brain damage from the beating I'd just taken from Wanda. I would jerk my head around like I had a tic taking place, but Wanda yelled out, "You better straighten up or I'll give you another dose." And guess what, that little old tic went right away. After all, Wanda was the Bare Knuckle Champ at our house in those days.

Trees a Plenty
Sid
1957

In 1957, we lived at the Ed Covington farm in southwestern Warren County just off the Nashville Road. It was a big farm by today's standards, approximately two hundred and fifty acres and almost perfectly flat. The Natcher Parkway went right through the middle of it and it's joined on the south side by W.K.U.'s Agriculture farm. While we lived there we milked cows, grew tobacco, and planted pine trees. In fact we planted ten thousand pine seedlings. It was pasture land mostly with a few acres of blackberry briars here and there. We laid off rows in ten foot squares with a mule and a turning plow. Then we used a steel rod with a foot rest on the side about ten inches up from the tip to poke a hole in the furrow. We then placed a seedling in the hole and made another hole right beside that one with the rod and with a round and round motion with the top of the rod we packed the soil against the seedling. This also left a hole for water to stand in to feed the seedling. It was slow and tedious work. While passing through a while back I noticed many of those trees are still there. The Covington Grove subdivision also has many of those tall pine trees still standing. It's good to see they saved most of those trees we planted when they developed that land. It's a bit of a wakeup call to see mature trees that are younger than I am, but also nice to know that God has seen fit to leave both of us still standing after all these years.

What's a Brother For
Glenn
1957

If you live in Kentucky I believe you are
more likely to be a smoker than in any other
state in the union. I'm not certain as to why that
is but I believe statistics will back me up. Maybe
it's because there is so much tobacco grown
here, or just maybe it's somehow gotten into our
genes over the years. It's obviously not smart to
smoke. You don't have to be an Einstein to
figure out that inhaling harsh smoke into your
lungs can't be anything but bad for you. My
father smoked all his adult life and died of a
heart attack at fifty one years old. He had a
leaky heart valve probably all his life and open
heart surgery wasn't being done in nineteen
sixty one when he died, but he may have lived
longer had he not smoked. I think most people
start smoking because they think it's cool and
not because it tastes good. If you smoke I'd urge
you to quit, and if you don't I would recommend
you never start.

At the time this event happened we were
living at Mrs. Becky Howell's place.

Looking back, I believe Glenn was really
trying to teach me a lesson when one afternoon
he gave me the high sign and went out the back
door. Of course I followed him very discretely out
behind the smokehouse. When we rounded the
corner he peeked back around to see if the coast
was clear like a private detective suspicious of

being followed. Boy, this had to be something good as careful as he was being. When he was satisfied it was all clear he reached in his pocket and produced a cigarette and a match. "Want to smoke one with me?" he asked. "But of course my good man, I'd love to," I told him. So he handed me the cigarette and lit me up. He stood there a minute and then told me he had forgotten something and that he'd be right back and for me to go ahead and enjoy my smoke. That's cool with me so I back up to the smokehouse, prop one foot up against the wall and proceeded to enjoy myself between fits of coughing. All of a sudden I hear Glenn say, "See there Daddy, Sid's smoking that nasty old cigarette he got out of your pack!" And sure enough, I look around and here comes Daddy already pulling his belt out. That's such a sickening sound, that chu-chu-chu-chu sound that leather makes being withdrawn from belt loops at a high rate of speed. Needless to say my cigarette wasn't the only thing smoking when Daddy finished with me.

I didn't even try to explain that Glenn was the one that set this all up. Since I was certain he just did it for my own good. Yeah right! Oh well--I too have had my moments!

Heading for the House
Steve
1958

Throughout the southern states and
especially Kentucky, the countryside is dotted
with small country churches and deserted
country store buildings. If you drive the back
roads of our state, you'll seldom go more than
two or three miles without seeing one or two of
these little churches and just about everyone of
them are still holding worship services and
Sunday school as well as prayer meeting or Bible
studies on Wednesday night. Transportation
being what it was before the advent of
automobiles, it was a much smaller world we
lived in. You were much more likely to walk to
different places in those days than you are now.
A short time back I actually knew a guy who
bought a motor scooter to ride to the mailbox
that was no more than seventy five feet from his
front door and he could walk as well as anybody.
He just didn't want to.

Years ago, many people walked to church,
which brings me to this story.

Neither my Daddy nor Momma ever drove
a car so the only times they went to church
regularly was when we lived within walking
distance of a country church. We were living at
the Ben Hewitt place on Cemetery Road. Our
house was no more than two hundred yards
away from the Cassidy Free Will Methodist
Church. We were raised as Baptists but Daddy

always said he figured God could find a feller wherever he went to church, no matter what name was over the door. That sounds like a pretty simple assessment to me and I'll go with that. My little brother Steve enjoyed going to Sunday school at Cassidy maybe a little more than he enjoyed the Worship Service or preaching as we called it. One particular Sunday, Steve had gone to church by himself and as soon as Sunday school was over he started running across the church yard toward home. His Sunday school teacher saw him leaving and she called out to him and asked him if he wasn't going to stay for preaching? He never slowed up but yelled back at her, "No I'm not. Momma was making a banana pudding when I left and I want to get back home before it's all gone." If you had ever had Momma's banana pudding you would most likely cut Steve some slack for skipping the preaching and heading for the house. The banana pudding didn't usually last long around the Croslin household.

A Croslin Kind of Christmas

Christmas time has always been special to our family for several reasons. I think our Daddy was the real cheerleader when it came to Christmas. He had spent many lonely Christmas seasons as an only child, living with a very old couple that raised him. He never got much of anything for Christmas himself, and he always tried to make it as special as he could for us. I remember there was always all the fruit we could eat, as well as hard candy. Daddy always found a way to get his hands on a whole stalk of bananas every Christmas. We each got one a day for as long as they lasted. My sister Barbara wonders even to this day where in the world Mamma kept the bananas hidden. We didn't live in a forty room mansion, but more like a four or five room house, and that didn't offer all that many hiding places. It had to have been close to the stove, otherwise they would have frozen, and it will always remain a mystery for her I guess. Our stockings were one of Daddy's wool socks, and the apple would always be in the toe, followed by an orange and some lemon drops, plus a couple of peppermint candy canes with the crook always hanging over the top.

My brother Glenn and I one year got a cap pistol each and they were the coolest guns you ever laid eyes on. The grips were white with a black, long horn steer head on each side. The holsters were black with those little round gem stones in green and yellow and red and if you didn't want to get shot full of holes, you just better not mess with them two Croslin boys. We would have the house stinking like a sulphur well from all those caps going off. We were allowed to shoot only one roll of caps each inside the house, and after that, to the yard we went. One year, Glenn even got a Red Rider hat and a pair of gloves with the fringe on the cuff. He was such a showoff in those we could hardly stand him. He'd walk kind of hip shot back and forth in front of the mirror and cut his eyes around to the side trying to see his own profile. It's not a good idea to look off to the side when you're being faced down in the middle of the street in a gunfight, profile or not! He even tied his holster down with a shoestring like the bad boys in the movies did. We stomped a few salmon cans till they curled up onto our heels for boot heels. We never had cowboy boots so we improvised and we were bad!

I remember one year, Glenn got a basketball for Christmas and I got a goal. We wore the ground down at least three inches deep around the front of the smokehouse where we nailed up our goal.

I learned to make some prodigious hook shots, for that's the only shot I could get off without him blocking it. We played hours upon hours with brown jersey gloves on and occasionally had to sweep the snow off before we could play. The girls always got a doll of some kind, and they took much better care of their stuff than we boys did, or maybe it's just really hard to wear out a doll. My sister Wanda kept all her dolls just like new. It was really sad when they all burned in the house fire in fifty four. Even though we had some really fun times at Christmas with the toys we got, still the best part of it was going to town and looking at all the Christmas lights. My sister, Elizabeth, had the prettiest house I've ever seen at Christmas, when she put a string of those big, soft glow, blue lights around her picture window. Other than a cedar tree with lights and some icicle, that's all the decoration she ever had, and it was beautiful!

Later on, we made our own decorations out of biscuit can ends. We'd cut the paper off of them, punch a hole through the edge, and glue some glitter to the little shiny disks, and hang them on the tree with fine wire or thread. To an outsider, they probably looked about as tacky as a woman with hairy arm pits, but we liked them and enjoyed making them.

Daddy and Momma never gave each other gifts at Christmas, but the older kids always got each of them something. I never was able to get my Daddy anything for Christmas, even though I wanted to get him a new pocket knife, for he set great store in having a good knife! I did get to enjoy giving my Momma many gifts over the years.

We never had a bad Christmas until Daddy died and it was a long time before we learned to enjoy it again. The same thing was true when in seventy nine our brother Robert died, and Jeanne's oldest son Johnnie was killed in a car wreck on Christmas Eve. Time is a good healer and in time we again enjoyed our Christmas get-togethers. When Momma died in ninety seven, our Christmas get-together started to lose its luster to some of the family members, and they wanted to stop having them. It had gotten to be a hardship I suppose on the younger ones, to try to make the rounds in their spouse's families, so we stopped. Christmas Night will always be a downer to me after such great times we had together as a family on that night.

Bad Soup
Robert
1958

Our Momma was one of the best cooks you ever saw. She could take what some folks would call rough grub such as pinto beans cooked with some jowl bacon or a ham hock, along with fried potatoes, and cornbread and you were in tall cotton as we used to say. I used to tell people we had hundreds of good things to eat growing up and they were all pinto beans. But Momma was a genius at making something really tasty out of pretty much nothing. When we had biscuits left over from breakfast which didn't happen often, she would make what she called a cold biscuit pudding with them. She would crumble them up in a pan, pour in some milk, some sugar, a little vanilla flavoring, and some butter and bake it. You needed a football helmet on when you were eating this to keep your tongue from slapping your brains out. It was what we called larruping! I imagine there were lots of recipes like that, handed down through the years so as not to waste anything that could be used. I'm sure some restaurants and cafes use this practice and that's fine if you know what you're doing.

I remember Momma always made the best soup you ever tasted, whether it was bean soup, vegetable soup, or vegetable beef soup, and as my brother Tommy would say "it was stomp down good." One Saturday night, my brother Robert came home from a night on the town and he may have been slightly intoxicated as well as being hungry. He helped himself to a big pan of soup he found on the table. After dipping up a bowl full he crumbled it full of crackers, dusted it good with black pepper like he did to just about everything and sat down to eat. He ate about a half a bowl and that was all he could stand. He got up and went on to bed. The next morning at breakfast he told Momma that was the worst pot of soup she had ever made. She looked at him kind of funny and he said, "Momma, I'm sorry but it just wasn't good." The reason she looked at him funny was she hadn't made any soup lately and asked him what in the world he was talking about. He said, "The soup you left for me on the kitchen table last night." My Momma was dumbfounded for a minute, and then she broke into an absolute laughing fit. We all started laughing too just because Momma was, and we didn't even know what she was so tickled about. Come to find out, Ol Robert had eaten a bowl of dirty dish water Momma had forgotten to throw out the night before and had left it setting on the table. From then on he was much more careful and checked everything out before he chowed down.

The Nectar of the Woods
Sid and Glenn
1958

Kentucky is a very versatile state. A farmer can just about pick and choose to grow any crop he desires. The soil is well suited to most types of grains, legumes, grasses, and we are blessed with a long growing period. Farmers begin planting some crops in March and the growing season lasts until frost in mid October. A study a few years back concluded that Kentucky's soil was very well suited for the growing of grapes for wine making. I could have told them that way back in 1958.

People have been making wine in Kentucky for many, many years. The more popular wines have been made from grapes, blackberries, strawberries, and elderberries. These were inexpensive to buy or even free because they grew wild here in the Commonwealth, which helped to aid in their popularity. I've been told they were very excellent in flavor and bouquet, as well as packing a considerable punch. Kentuckians who over-indulged in these wines have been known to fall out of a basement, but they sure smelled nice when they finally came to rest.

The late summer of fifty eight found us living on the Cemetery road at the Porter Meeks Place. It was a pretty little farm that backed up to a high bluff overlooking the beautiful Barren River. It had a nice apple orchard and a pond with lots of pond cats which is a catfish that never gets very big due to overpopulation, unless the Croslin family lived close. There was work to do most of the time with tobacco to grow and the usual farm chores, but occasionally we had some slack time. We were seldom ever at a loss for something to amuse or entertain ourselves with. We made our own fun.

My older brother Glenn and I was a couple of enterprising young men even at nine and thirteen years old. We had an eye for business. One day we were brainstorming for a money making venture, and we hit upon the perfect plan. We would go into the wine making business. Why not, other people had done it in California and even as far away as France, and Italy, and we figured if it worked well there it would work just as well here in Warren County, Kentucky. Just across the road from our house was a small thicket with wild grapes growing in just about every tree all the way to the top. Bushels and bushels of wild Possum grapes were there for the taking. They were a much smaller grape than the concord variety but were loaded with juice and possums loved them, hence the name. Our business plan was simple. Make all we could, drink all we could and sell the rest, for a small nominal fee of course. We got Momma's dish pans, which happened to have quite a bit of sugar in one of them, and lit out for the vineyard. With our enthusiasm running wild, we started picking grapes with both hands till we had enough gathered to run off our first batch. We used our hands to squeeze the juice out into one of the dish pans. Our first run was approximately one quart. We added the sugar till we figured we'd better stop until we had our first wine tasting so as not to get it too sweet or have Momma wondering what happened to all her sugar. We capped off our first batch by 9:00 A.M. It was beautiful when held up to the sunlight. You couldn't see through it with a flashlight. We began talking about distribution and market share and all those other things that wine makers talk about, and what all we would buy with the money once we were up and running at full speed.

The first thing you know it was 3:00 P.M. and our wine had already aged six hours. We decided that was plenty long enough for wine to age, so we went to the smokehouse where we had stored our wine, and each one tried a sip. "Not too bad, is it, partner?" I asked and Glenn agreed with me wholeheartedly. So, we pretty much killed that quart of possum grape wine right off the bat. We agreed we should keep this strictly confidential between the two of us in order to stave off any competition for as long as possible.

It wasn't too long before Glenn excused himself from the staff meeting and started ambling off toward the privy. I passed him in a dead run undoing my bibbed overalls as I went. When I say as I went, that's exactly what I mean. I had committed a most embarrassing foul up. By the time I got to the privy, I didn't need to go any longer. I always was a more sensitive child than he was. As I started back to the house, he nearly ran over me in his haste. Had a man on a motorcycle offered him a ride, he would have said "No thanks, I'm in a hurry!" Yes sir, we were up and running at full speed all right! It went on like that all afternoon and well into the evening before things finally started getting back to normal. We were plumb worn out from all the running we had done.

Later that night when we were in bed, we hit upon the absolute perfect plan. We would produce a laxative that was dirt cheap, and we would even guarantee it to work while you were in deep, peaceful slumber. Our laboratory studies had proved it! After all that, we had to invent something to remove purple stain from the hands and arms. We had a regular little cottage industry going there.

Put it Away for a Winter Day
All of us
1959

If you pay attention to nature, you'll notice that animals that live off of perishable foods that are left unprotected, store up for the winter while their particularly favorite food is in season. For example the squirrel gathers and stores nuts in hollow trees as well as digging a hole in your flower beds and stashing food there. I've seen squirrels dig through six inches of snow to get to nuts they have buried. It's a matter of survival for the squirrel, and my family operated on the same principle. "Put it away for a winter day" was Phillip and Julia's motto.

We started every year by planning and planting a big garden. As sharecroppers, it was part of the deal we could grow as big a garden as we wanted and it was all ours. In 1959, we put out our normal early garden such as potatoes, cabbage, radishes, beets, onions, and peas. Then as the ground warmed around the first of May, we planted corn, tomatoes, squash, beans, and okra. And as an insurance policy against dry weather or some other circumstance, we put out a late garden, so it was a process for sure. When the first vegetables were ready to harvest, we began to preserve or home can. While our Momma worked as a nurse's aide, we gathered, cleaned, cut up, and made ready all the produce she could can that evening. My sisters had supper ready when she got home and as soon as she finished eating she began canning and didn't stop till it was all in the jar. We continued this all summer long and every one of us was involved. We also ate fresh vegetables every day straight from the garden. The only thing we usually had to buy was meat and flour, sugar, coffee, and tea. Everything else we grew ourselves.

Daddy built shelves in the cellar that summer all the way around the walls and from the floor to the ceiling and we filled it up with canned vegetables. There were hundreds and hundreds of quarts and pints of food. The potatoes were put into a trench we had dug in the ground and lined with straw, then a fine layer of lime was dusted over them topped by another layer of straw and the process was repeated till the potatoes were all stored. By summer's end we were prepared to weather the storms of winter.

I don't remember which one of us discovered it but the unspeakable had happened to us again. The shelves holding all our canned food had collapsed. It was like it imploded with everything being pulled to the center and breaking the jars as they crashed together. Of the hundreds of cans of food we had in that cellar, only about thirty or forty weren't broken. It was one of the few times in my life I ever saw my Momma cry over anything other than a death of a friend or a family member. But she cried that day not only for all the hard work we had put into it, but with the realization that we had lost an entire winter's food supply in one

instant. That lost food, someway or somehow would have to be replaced, and she didn't know just how that was going to be accomplished. Daddy was a pretty good carpenter and I doubt it was due to his workmanship that caused the collapse for he had braced it up very well.
We got through it by eating lots more pinto beans and potatoes than we had planned on that winter. Fortunately, we all liked beans and potatoes and never got sick of eating them like you might some foods. Also, word got around that if you saw a rabbit run across the road in front of you, you had best slam on your brakes quick for you could bet there would be a Croslin right behind him.

Momma Gets Down
Julia
1960

I remember back in the late fifties or early sixties there were dance shows on T.V. that were tremendously popular. Our sister Wanda felt like she just couldn't miss one of them, for she had always loved to dance. She would try to get one of us boys to be her dance partner, and we didn't care about doing that under any circumstances. So she'd do all the new dance steps like "The Twist," or the other dances that were popular at the time by herself. She really thought she could tear up jack on the dance floor, and was always ready to show us how good she was at it. I wouldn't have told her I thought she was a good dancer for anything in the world for fear I'd have to dance with her, but she really was good!

One day she was dancing while we watched it on television, and Momma came through the room. Wanda said, "Come on, Momma! Let's show them how it's done on the dance floor." Momma said, "I would, but I don't know these new dances you kids are doing now days." One of us popped off, "Wanda, leave her alone because you know she can't dance." Momma turned around and glared at us for a second, and then commenced to do the Charleston like you wouldn't believe. She was tearing it up like new ground. We were hollering, and whooping, and laughing like crazy, as she went around the room a couple of times and then danced her way off into another room. We could hear her laughing from the other room. Then, it hit us! We had never before seen our Momma dance. We had heard her tell about going to dances when she was a kid, but that was ages ago. You're not supposed to do that sort of stuff after you've had eleven kids. I wonder why some kids think their parents are "Old Fogies" with little life left in them after a certain age, but we too were guilty because that was our Momma!

We worried Momma to death trying to get her to dance for us after that, but she seldom ever would. I even told her I'd dance with her, but not where Wanda could hear me. Our Momma could get down!

Hell Hath No Fury as a New Kid That's Scared Sid
1961

We moved to Richardsville on New Year's Day of 1961. There was about six or eight inches of snow on the ground and really cold--just a wonderful day to move to what we thought at the time was the end of the earth. But remember, we were old pros at this moving business. My Momma cooked dinner at one place, and supper at the other and everything was put away in its proper place. Every   picture hung, every bed made, and even a spot picked out for a garden and a basketball court. I'm here to tell you we were organized and ready to go!

My first day at Richardsville School left a lot to be desired. My fifth grade teacher was Mrs. Fairy Runner and she was a very sweet lady to me and tried hard to make me feel welcome there as did all the other kids, but for one exception. At lunch time, I sat at a table and ate by myself until this one big kid came over and sat down. I said hi to him and I was thinking here may be a new friend, until I saw the sick little smirk of a grin on his face. He said, "I'm going to cut your guts out at recess," then he got up and left. I had just come from a school where there were no bullies or really mean kids, and I was terrified of this goofball. At recess, I stayed close to the school and the teacher, but I could see him looking at me from the playground when he wasn't pushing some kid around that was smaller than him. Thankfully, I was able to avoid him the rest of that day, but I could hardly sleep that night for thinking bout it. I should have told Daddy about it, but I just couldn't bring myself to do it and have him thinking I was a chicken.

All night long I thought about what I should do, and the only thing I knew for sure was if I didn't face this doofus, I would be a marked man from that time on. So, the next morning at recess, I went down to the basketball court and was watching the other boys shoot hoops. It didn't take him long to spot me and here he came. I had a plan of action in mind and as soon as he got within reach, I hit him dead in the nose as hard as I could hit him and the blood started flying. I have never before or since felt a rage like I felt that day on the playground, and I showed him no mercy. He outweighed me by forty pounds I guess, and at twelve years old that's a lot. I rained blows on his head as fast as I could and as hard as I could. I put about twenty dollars' worth of nickel knots on his head. I kept the barrage up until the bell rang and we went inside. I told him I'd be waiting that afternoon at recess and we could pick up right where we left off. I went to Mrs. Runner and told her the whole story including the threat the day before. She put her arm around my shoulder and told me, "Don't you worry about it; I'll take care of it." I never heard another word about it, and that afternoon he was the one that hung around close to the school house and the teacher. Evidently, I wasn't the first kid he had ever messed with, but I don't remember him having trouble with any others while I was there. I never had another problem with him after that, but I also never completely took my eye off of him after that either. I've never been proud of that incident because it should never have happened in the first place.

I believe I know what goes through these kids minds that are bullied in school these days, until they snap and do something really drastically wrong. I know I felt it that day many years ago. You see, I wasn't just fighting for myself. I was fighting against the kind of overbearing, hateful, mean kid that he was. Now why he was that way, I'm not sure. Maybe he wasn't loved or cared for properly, and was striking out for no other reason than that. I guess I'll never know why he did it. All I know for sure is I hope to never again feel the rage that I felt that day because I know now just how dangerous it can be.

The Proper Way to Decline an Invitation
Glenn
1961

Glenn was smooth as silk when it came to getting around Daddy. I believe he had read one of those self help books that teach you how to manage your boss. That was not the easiest thing in the world to do. Daddy's requests were usually not open for discussion period. But Glenn had always had more success in that regard than any of us, and it was a great source of pride for him.

Daddy was a smoker but he never bought cigarettes by the carton for some reason, and he was prone to running out of smokes, as he called them. If I live to be one hundred years old, I won't forget this day I'm about to describe. Daddy had run out of smokes and since he didn't drive a car, he would send one of us boys to the store for a pack of Camels. As a reward for going to the store he would buy us a treat of some kind. It was pretty hot that day, the 23rd of July nineteen sixty one, and Daddy said, "Pomp, get on your bicycle and ride over to Mr. Hudson's and get me a pack of smokes and I'll buy you a big R.C cola." Mr. Hudson's little country store was about two miles from our house, and a pretty easy ride. But it was hot and Glenn didn't want to go. So, he said, "Aw Daddy, I don't want to. Make Sid go." Now remember, this was Glenn he was talking to and I figured I may as well get myself ready to go. But no, instead Daddy said "Now Son, you shouldn't say

I don't want to go. You should say Father I'd rather not." Now Glenn thought he was off the hook so he said, "Well, Father I'd rather not go." Boom, Daddy gave him one of those trademark patented "foot turned sideways" kicks in the butt. I thought maybe a jay bird might build a nest in Glenn's drawers before he came down, but when he did alight, he was on that bicycle burning that road up. It's a wonder I didn't get run over by a car laying in the middle of the road laughing at Glenn's rear end going out of sight hunched over that old bike. Now I know it's not a Christian thing to derive satisfaction out of seeing someone get punished, but then I wasn't a Christian at that time and it did me good. Boy, what a fine day for a ride!

Things Happen, Things Change, Forever
The Family
1961

Everything was going really well for us there at Richardsville until tragedy struck us again. It wasn't a fire this time. I'll never forget getting off the school bus that day, and seeing several cars in the drive. My nephew that lived with us then was about five years old, and came running to meet us and said, "Your Daddy is dead."

God, I still shiver when I think about that day so long ago now. They had not had time to come to school and pick us up after Daddy died. There was a blessing in that, because it gave us a little bit longer before we got such bad news. Even now, the picture is still so vivid in my mind, of going into the house where Momma was sitting on the sofa, broken hearted and crying, surrounded by family and neighbors. Me and Steve ran to her and she hugged us both at the same time. I remember her saying, "How in the world am I going to raise these children by myself?" Her only thoughts were concerning the safety and welfare of her children. Glenn had stayed after school for basketball practice and my brother Billy and my brother-in-law Jerry had gone to get him. When they returned, he joined us in holding onto Momma. I'm sure neither of us really understood the gravity of that day, and how our lives were never going to be the same after that. But we also didn't realize the bond that had always held us together through the tough times would only grow stronger.

Daddy had been helping a neighbor pick the outside three rows of corn by hand so the tractor and picker could get into the field without riding the corn over onto the ground. Daddy had a heart attack and just fell over without warning and that was it. He was gone from us at fifty one years old. He died doing what he had always done--working and helping out a neighbor in need of a hand.

That house held too many bad memories for Momma I suppose, and she just didn't want to stay there any longer. So we moved back into the Alvaton school district. My brother Glenn was in his first year of high school and didn't want to move again. So he begged Momma to let him stay with my sister Wanda and her husband Jerry Runner. That way he could finish high school at Richardsville. I guess Glenn was just tired of moving. They were happy to have him. Jerry was a part time farmer and a really fine man. Glenn helped on the farm to pay for his room and board. I never knew how he felt being separated from Momma, me and Steve. But it broke my heart, for we were best buddies. I never have told him that, but I think he has always known it. We have never stopped being close to this day. He eventually moved to Pike County to start a business and has never returned to Warren County to live. He now lives in Lancaster, Kentucky, a small town near Lexington.

Together Forever
Phillip and Julia
1929-1961

My daughter Amy interviewed Momma for a class project at W.K.U. a few years ago and in that interview she asked Momma about her and Daddy's courting days. Momma was a little reluctant to talk about it at first because she was such a private person. But Amy, being a chip off the old block, wouldn't give up until she had her talking about it. She said, "Well, Phillip had a really fine buggy and a good buggy horse and was a right good looking young man. He was also a real gentleman that loved to laugh." I'm thinking, why would she go out with a man in 1929 that still traveled by horse and carriage, when every other young fellow had a car? But then I think, if I was a girl in 1929 living out in the sticks like she did, I would have gone out with a man if he was riding a goat and had a patch over one eye, just to be going somewhere. But then I'm not like Julia. I have seen pictures of Momma and Daddy when they had been married only a little while and they were a very nice looking couple. Unfortunately all those pictures burned in the first house fire we had. They met at an ice cream supper at the old Robison School just off the Cemetery Road in Warren County. They were auctioning off pies and cakes and Daddy was able to buy Momma's chocolate pie. The bid winner got to share his pie with the lady that made it. Our Momma was one very fine pastry chef and Daddy was one very fine pastry eater. What with Momma being a good looking lady and a good pie maker that was enough to snare Phillip. Whatever Daddy had going for him must have worked, for they took in ice cream suppers and church socials together on a pretty regular basis after that. That's where most all country folks did their courting in those days. I've even been to one or two ice cream suppers myself, but I was much too young to court. The courtship budded into a full-blown romance and they were married in twenty nine. They took a train to New Albany, Indiana to get married. They stayed one night and came home. It was a short honeymoon but kind of romantic come to think about it. It was one of the few times they ever left the state of Kentucky.

They set up housekeeping while living with the Wrights, the couple that raised Daddy from an infant. I suppose it was a mutually beneficial arrangement since it gave Daddy and Momma a place to live and the Wrights needed someone to keep an eye on them as they were getting way up in years and in poor health. Daddy felt like he owed it to them, but it must have been hard on Momma for she would have wanted her own house, her own furniture, and her own things. Things were so different in those days when it came to displaying affection. The only open signs of love and affection between Daddy and Momma that I remember were, of him walking up behind her while she was cooking or busy doing something, and slipping his arms around her and hugging her with a little peck on the cheek. There was never any of this disgusting suck face, lip locking, moaning like your thumbs were caught in a vise type of thing. Just a gentleness they had with each other...

They had their moments when they disagreed or fussed with each other for certain, but we never heard it unless Daddy came home with a snoot full. She would light into him then pretty good for she hated drinking and hated it even worse when he did it. The best thing about his drinking was he didn't do it often and he wasn't a mean drunk. He just got a little happier than he normally was and even forgot he couldn't sing a lick, but it never stopped him from trying.

Phillip and Julia were together on this earth thirty one years. They worked shoulder to shoulder and side by side and about all they accomplished was having and raising eleven children that loved them and respected them. They never knew the comforts of a new home and new cars and all the things we think are so terribly important these days. They did however know the comfort of having each other to lean on through the most trying times imaginable. The Depression years, two house fires where they lost everything they owned, and the everyday hardships of being sharecroppers and having such a large family. I've seen disgust in their faces and worry in their eyes but I don't recall ever seeing them ready to throw in the towel and give up on each other or their children. They were tough people in a tough world and they worked their way through it together.

After Daddy died, our Momma never remarried even though she was only forty nine years old when he passed away. I don't think she ever stopped loving him or missing him and neither did we. I'm not sure about Daddy's spiritual condition when he died, but I do know he believed in God and Heaven and an eternal life. He was well read in the Bible, and could quote scripture. He would never let us dove hunt because he always said that doves were a bird of peace and shouldn't be killed. (There were a few times I've wished I had a dove in each hip pocket when I got crossways with him.) Our Momma was a Christian although she didn't go to church that much, because she was a nurse's aide and worked most Sundays, and didn't have transportation on the Sundays she was off, but I know she loved the Lord.

I truly believe they are side by side now and will always be together forever in Heaven and I pray every one of their children have their tickets punched to see them there. It's nice to think we might even have another one of our family get togethers!

Sixteen and Out
Sid
1962

Meanwhile, upon my return to Alvaton High School, things were different. My grades started to slip along with my attendance, and from that time on I had no interest in school. I played sick whenever I could, and just didn't much care, the days I did go to school. Maybe I needed counseling or an old fashioned Phillip Croslin butt whipping but I got neither one. Daddy was gone and nobody ever got counseling as far as I knew in those days. That got to be the "in thing" many years later. I failed a few classes, but never failed to advance with the rest of my classmates. This went on for the next few years .The only two classes that I really did well in were history and Industrial Arts. I loved to read and work with my hands and we had two excellent teachers in those classes. Mr. Henry Resch taught history and he loved teaching it as much as I loved learning it. I couldn't wait for his class every day. Mr. Ralph Davis taught Industrial Arts and I really enjoyed his class. I have heard since that woodworking is good therapy. Just make those shavings fly and you'll feel better. I believe that to be true because it did make me feel better. I made Momma a set of book ends that I still have today. We made ash trays, and serving trays and cutting boards. Thank God, I've never made any license plates. I was at odds with the school principal most of the time and felt like he singled me out whenever anything went wrong. As a matter of fact I started to really hate him and for forty years it just festered inside me. I had nothing good to say about him at all. But get this, a few years ago, I made peace with God, and got saved. About a month after that, I was in my shop working, and out of the blue, it came to me to forgive and forget any bad feelings I had toward that man, and I did. Since that day, I have sat and had breakfast with him and talked like we were old friends. I've even had him for a Rook partner at the old country store nearby. Powerful huh!

I decided as soon as I turned sixteen, I was quitting school and I did. Certainly not my Momma's wishes and she tried to get me to stay in school. But I saw no need to stay any longer doing something I saw as a waste of my time. It was a mistake but we make them from time to time and you just have to learn from it and go on. I held jobs in the home construction business as a helper laying ceramic tile. I worked as a carpet installer's helper and was even a Coca-Cola salesman for a while. There's nothing wrong with any of those jobs but there's not too much of an opportunity to grow. Next I went to work in an automotive parts manufacturing plant and hated it. I was ready to quit and had even decided I was quitting come Friday. I told this old fellow that I worked close to what I had decided to do. He put his hand on my shoulder and so quietly said, "Aw son, it'll get better, just give it a little time." It did get better and I stayed thirty two years. I worked my way up the ladder until I was the Customer

Quality Liaison, calling on just about every automotive assembly plant in the country and even Canada.

I Hope You Get Better Soon
Sid
1963

After my father died, Momma just didn't want to stay in that house any longer in Richardsville, so yep, you guessed it, we moved again. We found a pretty nice place just a couple of miles outside of Bowling Green. It was the nearest to town we had ever lived which made it handy if you wanted to go to town. It wasn't nearly as far to walk. We had a nice big yard and a real nice outside toilet. Man, we were moving on up in the world.

A Mr. James Rush lived across the road from us and I got acquainted with him. Come to find out, he had known my father for a long time. His wife Beatrice was an old classmate of Daddy's when they were just kids. They were the finest people you could ever want to meet. They had one son that was married and lived in Owensboro, Kentucky. I suppose I was kind of like a grandchild to them and they just about treated me that way. They also most likely felt sorry for me for having just lost my Daddy at such a young age. I began helping him on the farm for a mind boggling fifty cents an hour. Hey that was pretty good money for a kid on the farm in those days. I hauled hay, set tobacco, cut tobacco, housed tobacco and mowed his three acres of grass with a twenty inch push mower. It didn't matter, it all paid the same. He always furnished dinner which was a treat, for Beatrice was a world class cook.

Mr. Jim, as I called him, really filled the void left by my Daddy's death. He took time to teach me things like how to ride a tobacco setter, drive a pickup truck, mow hay, milk cows, throw the wickedest curveball you ever saw and smoke. That last one I wished he hadn't bothered with. His tractor had a bench seat which was wide enough for both of us to sit in. I got good at rolling cigarettes. I'd roll him one, and then one for me, while all the time bouncing like crazy on this tractor.

Along about this time I had started to learn to play a guitar. At least I knew three chords which would be plenty good enough to play all the bluegrass songs and most country songs at that time. I didn't have a guitar so anytime my brother Buddy came to visit, the first thing I asked him was did he have his guitar with him. He usually did because you just never knew when you might run up on a talent scout and he wanted to be ready just in case. He had shown me those first three chords.
That fall, Mr. Jim took the flu and was just about completely bedfast all winter. I helped him milk the cows morning and night and between milking he was in bed. One day after I had begged Buddy to let me keep his guitar for a day or two just in case any of those scouts happened to come by, I decided I would just take it over to Mr. Jim's and play him a few songs I had learned. A little music would surely make him feel better. He seemed like he enjoyed the first couple of numbers I did. I gave him my best shots right off the bat. But then I started to lose

his interest I suppose 'cause when he covered up his head I figured he had had all the entertainment he could stand in one day, him being so weak and all. So I got up, sacked up my guitar and said, "Mr. Jim, I hope you get better." He raised one corner of the blanket, peeped out and said, "I hope you do too Son, cause if we don't, neither one of us is going to make it!"

Years later Mr. Jim got cancer and was in really bad shape. I stopped to see him one day on my way home from hunting and we sat and talked a while about all the fun things we had done. His wife Beatrice had told me he had stopped eating. I asked him if there was anything I could do for him. He said, "If you were to kill a quail or two more than you want for yourself I would sure love to have one more to eat." I said, "I believe I can fix you right up Mr. Jim." I went to the truck and got four quail out of my hunting coat, dressed them and gave them to his wife. She had them in the skillet before I left that afternoon. She told me at his funeral a few days later those quail were the last meal he ate, and he had enjoyed them so much. It was the least I could do for an old friend.

Way to Go Croslin
Elizabeth
1964

My oldest sister Sarah Elizabeth was the first born in our family. There was nothing about her other than being pretty that would stand out about her other than her eyes. I always thought she had the prettiest big brown eyes that God ever put in the face of a human being. Unfortunately, she had the distinction of having been the oldest child as well as being born during the Great Depression. This meant she never got to enjoy being a child as much as she should have. As soon as she was big enough, she helped Daddy in the fields or Momma with the housework or watched the younger children while Momma worked in the fields. This just shouldn't be so, but it took everybody to make ends meet and eke out a living during the Depression. Of course this happened long before I was born, but I never once remember her saying she felt deprived or put upon with the hard work she did as a child.

Elizabeth had a fierce loyalty to her friends and her family and would have fought like a wildcat for either one. She supported every one of us in whatever endeavor we chose to follow. She was a huge sports fan and could just about flatten a softball when she was a kid. She swung for the fences with every at bat and encouraged us all to do the same. She agreed with the old adage, "Swing as hard as you can just in case you hit it."

When our brother Glenn was in his senior
year at Richardsville High School he had become
a pretty darn good basketball player. None of us
had gotten to see him play a lot and Momma
and Elizabeth had never seen him play at all
until the game between Richardsville and
Alvaton at the Alvaton gymnasium. Elizabeth
and her husband Kenneth picked us up and
took us to the ballgame. We all sat on the
visitor's side of the gym that night. Now all my
brothers and sisters had gone to school at
Alvaton but we supported kin more than Alma
Mater. It was one whale of a ball game and that
little old gym was rocking that night and so was
Glenn. He was playing his heart out for his
school no doubt, but more for his Momma and
the rest of his family. He scored twenty five
points that night and with every basket he made,
even if it was a free throw, Elizabeth would
stand up and scream, "Way to go, Croslin!" at
the top of her lungs with a special emphasis on
Croslin! She wanted that name indelibly etched
in everyone's memory, and believe you me, she
had some powerful lungs in those days. Had the
rest of us not been just as proud, we would have
been embarrassed by her screaming after every
single point he made.

If you're the son or daughter of a poor
sharecropper the chances you're going to have
something to stand up and cheer about are slim
to none so you take advantage of it when it does
happen. Glenn didn't score that many points
every night, but it may have been because he
never had his sister Elizabeth there cheering for

him either. Oh by the way, Alvaton won the
game that night, but we all got what we came for.
A chance to stand up and cheer for one of us!
Way to go Croslin!

They Must Be Rich
Barbara
1964

My sister Barbara married Jack Keyser, a
Yankee from Columbus, Ohio in nineteen fifty
two. He was the first Yankee that I had ever seen.
He was in the insurance business and in spite of
that he seemed to be a pretty nice fellow. But he
took my sister off to Ohio to live and I didn't
much like that. She only came home to
Kentucky about once a year. When they came to
visit they stayed with Roy and Ida Wright,
because we just didn't have room to put them
up at our house. I hardly knew my own sister
but in nineteen sixty four the company that
Jack worked for transferred him to Louisville,
Kentucky. When they moved to Louisville they
bought a beautiful home in the St. Mathews area.
This was the newest area in Louisville at that
time and mostly professional people lived there.
It was what we called the ritzy section of town.
Had we lived in Louisville, this is where we
would have peddled our blackberries.

So in sixty four she came to Bowling
Green and invited me and Steve to go home with
her and spend a week so we could get
acquainted. School was out and we decided to
give it a try. She seemed nice enough and she
had two children, Nancy and Kevin that we liked,
so why not go? They had a brand new sixty four
Chevy station wagon, and it was the first brand
new car I remember riding in. This was before I-
65 was finished all the way from Bowling Green

to Louisville. We had to travel about halfway on 31-W which was a two lane highway and it was about a three hour trip. Needless to say, by the time we got there this cat needed to find the sandbox. Gosh but they had a beautiful home--a new two-story brick with the prettiest grass I'd ever seen and fine furniture inside. I knew they were in the chips when we got inside and Barbara showed me the bathroom, which of course I needed to use. While standing there doing my business, I looked over on the bathroom counter and there was a bowl of candy, in one of those clear cut glass dishes. This just blew my mind. I'm thinking "these people must be rich." We got candy at home just every once in a while and here they even had it in the bathroom. These were coconut bonbons, pink, white, and yellow ones. Somebody had already eaten all the chocolate ones, so I decided to have one myself. I popped in a pink one, bit into it and damn if it wasn't soap. Now why in the world would anybody buy soap like that to just look at?

While visiting with Barbara, Steve and I got to experience eating our first charcoal grilled steak. I thought it was the best thing I ever tasted at the time and I still enjoy them. We also went to the golf driving range and hit golf balls. That was the first golf ball I had ever hit with a golf club. We usually hit them with a ball bat. We even went to the pool and swam all day. I was the king of the high dive. I did it like the boys down home when we swung off into the water from a rope tied in a tree top that hung out over the creek--I held my nose with one hand and my clackers with the other. I was drawing quite a crowd when Barbara showed up and said it was time to go. Now how's that for you, just as I was getting comfortable in front of a crowd.

Barbara and Jack went out of their way to show us a good time and I've always appreciated that very much. It also showed me it was possible to do well, even if you were just a sharecropper's son or daughter.

The Best There Ever Was
Momma
1964

When I was fifteen years old, my Momma told me one morning to catch a ride from school that afternoon with one of the teachers that lived in town. I was to meet her at the drugstore downtown on the square. I needed a haircut and we had done this before, so I never thought too much about it. When we met, she finished her coke and we started down the street. When we got to the corner of College and Park Row she said, "Let's go this way." Now, the barber shop was straight on up College Street, but we turned and went up a block to State Street. I didn't know where we were headed. When we get to State Street, we turned right. We walked about three blocks. When we got to Royal Music Co. we went inside. I had no idea why we there, but they had the walls hanging full of all kinds of musical instruments. On one end were used ones and the rest were all new. She said, "Now Kenny pick out the guitar you want." I was dumbfounded and I thought I hadn't heard her right. I said, "What do you mean?" She said, "I'm going to buy you a guitar."

Now I knew my mother made about sixty-five cents an hour as a nurse's aide in a nursing home and there was no way she could afford it. I asked her if she was serious and she said she was. So I picked a cheap used flat top guitar for thirty dollars. My Momma was no dummy when it came to musical instruments, and she said,

169

"Now Kenny, I know that's not the one you really want." I said, "Momma, this one is fine." She said, "Which one of the new ones would you like to have?" I knew there was no getting around her and maybe I didn't try hard enough. So I went to the one that first caught my eye when we walked in--a little red Gibson Melody Maker electric guitar. I told her that one was the one I wanted but it was too expensive for her to buy. Lord, it cost one hundred and seventy four dollars. She told the salesman, "We'll take that one." He said, "I'll throw in a case too, but you're going to need an amplifier. I have a nice little amp I can let you have for fifty dollars." She told me to wait while she made the arrangements. God, I couldn't believe this. I couldn't in my wildest dreams imagine what had just taken place. It wasn't too long until we were back on the street headed back to the drug store where my brother Buddy always picked her up after work--me and momma, side by side with me carrying my guitar and amplifier! I didn't know you could feel that good and that guilty at the same time about anything. I asked her why she would do such a thing. She never slowed her step, but told me, "Son, with your leg like it is, you may have to make a living someday with music and I wanted to make sure you had a way to do it." Now how's that for you?

I had never given a thought to not being able to work because of my leg. It never had kept me from doing anything I wanted to do before. But that was Momma; she was born to worry. I've no idea how long she had thought that over before that day, but knowing her it probably had been on her mind for a long time. To think about what she did every day in taking care of the elderly people in the nursing homes where she worked, changing messy beds, dirty diapers on old folks and the heavy lifting of patients in and out of beds for sixty five cents an hour and to take that money, and spend it on a guitar for me is incredible. But that was Momma. She thought of everybody else before herself. I've never made a living solely with music, but I have supplemented my income with it by playing and singing, and writing country songs. I even recorded in Nashville and they sold somewhere under a million--somewhere "way" under a million.

It is heartbreaking to see some of the disadvantaged kids today whose parents put themselves before their children's needs. God gave me a mother and later on a wife of the same cut of cloth. They're the best there ever was!

Oh, by the way, I still have both the guitar and the amp and also the wife of forty years. The Denver mint couldn't print enough money to buy them.

A Picture is worth a Thousand Tears
Sid
1964

I've seen dozens of old pictures of the one or two room schools that were prevalent here in Kentucky. The entire school's children and teachers would be posed standing on the steps of the school with the first graders up front, second graders behind them, and so on with the oldest kids on the back rows and teachers on the ends. You seldom ever saw a child smile in these pictures. They just stood there with their baggy clothes, either ashamed of them, or scared, or bored and wanting to go play. Quite possibly it was all of those reasons depending on which child it was. But some time or other over the years they became a little bit more personal. That's when they began photographing each child individually and selling packets of pictures. Eventually the old black and white photos were replaced with beautiful color prints and they obviously became more and more expensive, priced beyond reach for the poorer kids' parents to purchase. They started off with a really nice big eight by ten, then a couple of five by sevens, and on down to the wallet sized pictures. The entire packet would run you about twenty dollars. Maybe that doesn't sound like very much money today but back in those days that was a week's worth of groceries or maybe two week's worth if you were a sharecropper's widow making sixty five cents an hour as a nurse's aide in a nursing home.

My freshman year at Alvaton High School, my brother Steve and I were put on the free lunch program. That really helped my Momma because that was fifty cents a day she didn't have to come up with for me and Steve's lunches. All I had to do was eat, then start scraping other kids' plates into big metal garbage cans and when they were full, two of us free lunchers would carry them down to the hog lot where the F.F.A. class kept their hogs and dump it over the fence to them. Then we washed and disinfected the cans with bleach before taking them back to the cafeteria for the next day's garbage collection. Next, we went back to the cafeteria and got the milk cartons and napkins we had sorted during the plate and tray scraping process as well as any other cafeteria trash. This all went down to the burn pile where we lit it and watched it burn until there was no danger of fire getting out. I never noticed it but we probably smelled of trash smoke when we got back to class. There were a couple of places in the school where they kept trash cans and all the teachers put discarded materials in them. These cans could get pretty heavy at times, and our custodians Mr. Rohmer Cosby and his wife Mrs. Ethel, who were pretty well on in years, just couldn't handle them. So us free lunchers would pick those up and take them to the burn pile.

The school pictures that year that were unsold had all been turned back in. I had stalled as long as I could on returning mine in hopes of by some small miracle we might come up with the money to buy more than just one three by five picture, since mine had turned out quite good that year, but my little miracle didn't happen. I never had given it a thought as to what happened to the unsold pictures until the day we picked up the big trash cans to dispose of its contents. When we poured out one of the cans onto the trash fire, right on top of the heap were my pictures I had returned the day before. I just stood there and watched them slowly curl up from the heat before bursting into flames. I could have saved them with no trouble at all, and took them home that afternoon but for some reason those pictures had lost their shine. I guess I was just too proud or maybe I thought it would be stealing if I salvaged the school's pictures. It's a good thing the smoke was thick and stinging our eyes because otherwise I would have had to explain to the other free luncher why I was crying. Later, much later, I realized my little miracle did happen, but I was just too proud or honest to take advantage of it!

Down and Out
Steve
1966

Our baby brother Steve went to visit
Tommy for a couple of days. At the time, Tommy
lived on the Covington farm right next to the
Bowling Green Warren County Airport. This was
a big cattle farm and it had quite a bit of tobacco
base. Tommy grew the tobacco and took care of
quite a big herd of beef cattle.   He was kept
pretty busy just about all the time with putting
up hay, raising the tobacco and taking care of
the cows. While he was working, there just
wasn't a lot for Steve to do. So, one day Steve
asked Tommy if he could drive his old sixty one
Ford convertible around on the farm. It had been
wrecked pretty bad in the front end and was no
longer fit for the highway. Tommy thought, what
can it hurt? It's junk anyway. So he gave Steve
the keys and gave him the usual be careful
warning and away he went. Tommy went back to
work in the tobacco patch. After a while he
thought he heard the car horn blowing. He
stopped work to listen and sure enough it was
Steve blowing the horn non-stop. Oh God, he's
turned it over on him sure as the world. Why oh
why did I let him drive that car, Tommy was
thinking, as he jumped on the tractor and tore
out for where the sound was coming from. At the
back side of the farm there was a low spot of
about an acre where at one time a pond had
probably gone dry. Tommy was going so fast on
that tractor across that rough pasture he could
hardly stay in the seat. Filled with dread he

headed for the only spot the car could be since it wasn't in sight. All kinds of pictures flashed through his mind and not one of them was good. He pictured the car overturned and Steve pinned under it, crushed. How in the world could he face Momma with this news? "I have killed your baby boy!" When he came to the edge of the low area where he could see, there Steve sat, top rolled back, radio blasting, sunglasses on, arm propped up on the back of the seat, and one hand on the horn blowing for Tommy to bring him some gas. Relief flooded over him until he wanted to just get off the tractor and thank the Lord that Steve wasn't hurt. Then he started thinking, "How in the world am I going tell Momma I have beaten her baby boy to death?"

Smoking From Both Ends
Sid
1965

At Alvaton High School, there were several boys that smoked, and when the bell rang to end a class, you had five minutes to get to the next class. If you ran really fast you could usually get a few puffs before you had to butt it out and get to the next class. All the boys went behind the Ag Building or the Shop as we called it, to do their smoking. All the teachers knew what they were doing, but as long as they weren't late for class they just let it slide. This worked for everyone unless it was raining. In case of rain, most of us just did without our smokes and waited for better weather.

Phillip Dearing, Gerald Stubblefield, and I decided we just couldn't wait for the weather to clear up, so we went down to the boiler room to have a quick one. It was nice and warm down there, not to mention being dry as well. We were talking about the smoking facilities we had discovered and how much more accommodating they were compared to the shop, when we heard a noise behind us. We turned in unison and were staring face to face, and eyeball to eyeball, with the school principal, Robert Morgan. We all three knew the jig was up and we were in trouble. He said "I want to see you three gentlemen in my office in about three minutes, if not sooner." I felt like we would get some consideration for being there two and a half minutes early, but he soon dispelled any notion of that. He came in and sat down, and just looked at our sorry selves standing alongside the wall in front of his desk. You could cut the tension in that little office with a knife. Finally, he said, "Mr. Dearing, I suppose your parents could afford to buy your cigarettes, but you certainly don't need to smoke, especially on school property." Phillip, who was an extremely nervous guy on a normal day but was a quivering blob by this time, agreed with him emphatically. Next he turned his attention to me and said, "Mr. Croslin, I'm pretty certain your mother can't afford for you to smoke anywhere and especially on school property." I just said, "Yes sir," not mentioning the fact that I bought my own smokes. He stared at me for a while and I begin to think we might get paroled, without getting any harsh punishment. He then turned to Gerald Stubblefield, who everyone just loved to death, and said, "Mr. Stubblefield, I don't know if your parents can afford for you to smoke or not." That's when Gerald interrupted him, right in the middle of his speech and said, "No, it doesn't bother them at all because I bum all my cigarettes." It was the worst thing to say at the worst possible time and I felt the noose draw tight around our necks. In order to save time, I just turned around and bent over his desk waiting for what I knew was coming, and he didn't disappoint. Five licks later I was out of there, and on my way to the next class. I could hear the other two low lives getting their rewards as I went down the hall. When I got to my class, I was about two minutes late for it. The teacher asked me why I was late and I said, "Aw, Mr. Morgan and I have been talking about a problem

I've been having with my tobacco." She seemed to be satisfied it was alright, since I had been talking to the Principal about what she guessed was an F.F.A. project, and I didn't see the need to elaborate any farther.

If Momma had only Known
Buddy
1966

I started playing guitar when I was twelve years old and by the time I was sixteen I could play pretty well. My brother Buddy was always stopping by the house saying "Sid, get your guitar and come on." I never asked questions, I just got my gear and loaded up. We usually went to one of his friend's houses where some pickers were gathered to have a jam session. I always enjoyed these for some of them were really quite good musicians and Buddy was a heck of a singer. One particular afternoon he came by the house, picked me up, and we drove into town. He didn't say where we were going and I didn't ask. That would turn out to be a huge mistake on my part. He pulled up to the curb in front of the roughest beer joint in Bowling Green. They had a head hulling there almost every night. I figured he was just going to run in and pick up some beer to go. When he got out of the car I just sat there. He stuck his head in the window and said "Come on, were playing here tonight." I said, "You're crazy, I can't go in there at my age." "Aw come on, they won't mind you playing here as long as you just don't drink anything," he said. Against my better judgment, I went along with it and that was another huge mistake. We went inside, set up our meager little bit of equipment and got started. Two of Buddy's friends were playing with us and after a while I started to relax. Everybody was enjoying themselves and the music was pretty good. We had just started the second set when this old boy came up to the bandstand and asked if I could play "Buckaroo," a huge instrumental hit at the time by Buck Owens and his band The Buckaroos. This was one of my favorite songs and I was pretty hot at playing it. I said, "Sure I'd be happy to play it for you." He stuck out his hand and when I shook hands with him he left a five dollar bill in my hand. I couldn't believe it. Here I was getting paid five dollars to play one song three minutes long when I usually got four dollars for hauling hay all day. Now this is what I need to be doing I thought. I had arrived in the big time. We took off on Buckaroo and man I was wearing it out when I heard a noise that sounded like a light bulb breaking. I look up just in time to see this guy falling backwards holding his head. Somebody had hit him in the noggin with a beer bottle, and just that quick the war began. Everybody in the place was fighting. Men, women, all of them were just hitting who ever got close. I said to myself, "Momma I love you and I'm sorry I've gotten myself killed in a beer joint." I asked one of the guys in the band what we were supposed to do. He stuttered when he got excited and he said, "You... you... you... you stay in this corner and if... if... if... if anybody gets close to... to... to you try to ki... ki... kill them with your gui... gui... guitar." He then put his guitar in the case, stepped off the bandstand and waded into the middle of the fight. The only thing he liked better than playing music was fighting and he was a much better fighter than a picker. When he hit somebody, they would lie down and take a nap. Finally we were able to get out a side door and get in the car just as we heard the sirens coming. I never believed the police were in that big of a hurry to get there anyway. Buddy said, "I'll be right back" and started back inside. I yelled, "Where are you going you fool?" He kept walking back inside where the fight was still going on. In a minute he came back out, got in the car just as the police rounded the corner and as we were driving away he handed me eight dollars. That was my share for nearly getting myself killed. It was years before Momma knew about that little incident, and still she chewed my butt out good over it.

From that time on I made it a point to know where I was going and what I'd be doing when I got there and who I'd be doing it with! My life was much safer after that! God looks out for idiots!

The Big Dummy
Sid
1968

Kentuckians have always had a great sense of humor and nobody loves a practical joke better than they do, myself included. They can however get out of hand at times and can even come back to haunt you. Such was the case in sixty eight. It was a week before Halloween and if you're going to pull a joke on someone, it's better to not wait until October 31st to do it. It has more effect and is also easier to pull off without getting caught. A friend of mine, J.C. Woods, lived next door to us and he stopped at my house and said, "Let's do something to scare somebody." What a capital idea old buddy. Let's make us a dummy and lay it on the side of the road. So we two dummies made a dummy by filling a pair of jeans with leaves, dressed him up in a white shirt with a little red paint on it for effect, and put an old pair of boots on it. The head was a paper sack full of leaves and some more red paint and a baseball cap. We left no stone unturned in the making of our little man. So right after dark we took Elwood over on the Scottsville Road within sight of my house and laid him just off the shoulder of the road where the car lights didn't really give you a perfect view but you still couldn't miss him. We hadn't much more than got back to the house before a car went by, then slammed on the brakes, backed up, and then took off squealing tires. They stopped at the next house and ran inside. We were having a gay old time laughing our butts off until about fifteen minutes later, when every on duty police officer in Warren County was on the scene with blue lights flashing and sirens blasting. We didn't have volunteer fire departments then or they would have all been there too. Within minutes the traffic was backed up a mile in either direction. This is when I knew we had really brought on some trouble. I got sleepy all of a sudden and went to bed and it was only six thirty in the evening. I let it be known I didn't want to be disturbed under any circumstances by anybody, especially by anyone in uniform. The police saw right away it was a dummy and just kicked it apart and left it in the ditch. We laid low for a few days and I thought it was all over with until one evening after work, when my sister Jeanne told me the police had traced the laundry markings in the shirt back to my brother Glenn and he was in jail under a ten thousand dollar bond. Every bit of the blood ran out of my face and I felt myself getting sleepy again. She said Glenn had called and was waiting for me to come and make his bail. I thought we better take him a lot of supplies cause he's gonna be in there a long time, for I didn't have ten thousand pennies to my name at that time, much less ten thousand dollars. Well, in about an hour Glenn and his wife Donna showed up at the house and Boy I think I was glad to see him. I never thought to ask him how he got out of jail. He was really raking me over the coals and my smart-assed sister was helping him. Donna started feeling sorry for me and she finally told them to knock it off. I'd suffered enough. They broke into fits of laughter and I wanted to cry from relief.

I learned two things from this little episode that will stay with me forever. I will never ever do anything like that again and I will love Donna forever and ever for blowing the whistle on them and putting me out of my misery.

Kinfolks Calling
Sid
1969

Shortly after starting in the manufacturing job, I received a letter telling me that Uncle Sam wanted to check my health. Now wasn't that sweet of him to think of me like that? So in May of sixty nine I boarded a bus to Nashville Tennessee to be examined for the Army. This is the quickest way I know to lose your dignity. We were all stripped down to our nothings with a little bag around our necks that held our valuables. This line had about fifty guys in it and most of them tried to be wise guys that day. We went through a station where you stepped up on a set of weight scales with a measuring scale at the back to get your height. I told this army doctor that my right leg was one and a half inches shorter than my left and which leg should I stand on. I can really be a big dummy at times and he said, "That don't make a damn. You will weigh the same either way!" That told me that even if you had the palsy you were fit for the Army in 1969. They would just put you to sifting flour in the kitchen. God, but that was embarrassing. Guess what? I passed the physical as did all but one and that poor old boy was about three fries short of a happy meal. I was only two fries short, so I was pronounced fit for the service. Within ninety days everyone I knew that had been examined that day was in the Army and on their way to Vietnam pretty soon. Over the next two years I only received one questionnaire from the Selective Service. Then the draft lottery was drawn and I drew a really high number and that was that. I was ready to go and would have done my duty without a doubt, but I never heard another word from the Army. Who knows, maybe we had moved so often they just couldn't catch up to me. I may still have an induction notice floating around somewhere in Warren County, Kentucky.

The Best of Times and the Worst of Timing
Sid
1969

In the spring of nineteen sixty nine I was in Bowling Green one night, sitting at the Dairy Bar having a late night snack, when two friends I had gone to school with pulled up beside me. After chatting from car to car for a while, my friend Linda said, "Hey. I know someone that wants to go out with you." I instantly wondered what sort of deranged person that could be. She was probably on the run from the law and needed some fast transportation. But being polite and really curious as to whom she was talking about, since I was not used to having girls just aching to be in my presence, I asked her who? She said, "Linda Stubblefield." I knew instantly that I was interested. Remember the little girl with the finger curls that bounced up and down as she walked? I perked up and said sure, I'd like that. She said maybe we could double date the next weekend. I said that sounded great to me. I knew I wouldn't have a scheduling conflict without even checking my date book, if I had had a date book. Since I hadn't seen her in about four years, I began to wonder what she was like now. She had always been shy in school and super smart, which gave us at least one thing in common. I too was shy in school. She was in the top five in G.P.A. her senior year at Alvaton. I had been the dropoutatorian my junior year. Sounds kind of like water and oil huh. She was in her second year at Western Kentucky University. Oh well, it would be good to see her just one more time. I didn't know it at the time, but our friend had told her the same story she told me, that she knew somebody that wanted to go out with her. I suppose she did it more as a favor to me than anything else. Who knows, but the thing is, it worked. She agreed to a double date. When we got to her house she came right out to meet me and God did she look great. So petite, pretty, and well dressed. Next to her, I felt like an outhouse in the lobby of the Waldorf Astoria. But she seemed genuinely glad to see me again. We had a great time that night. We went to a drive-in movie and had burgers and fries afterward. All through the movie I tried to get up the nerve to kiss her and not until the end did I do it. We were in the front seat of my buddy's Mustang and just as I leaned around to kiss her they turned the lights on all over the parking lot. It was lit up like a night game at Yankee stadium. I was in such a hurry I even missed her lips. I kissed her right smack dab on the chin. How embarrassing for both of us! I eventually got the nerve up to ask her out the following weekend, and she surprisingly agreed to go. I had a sixty four Ford Fairlane at the time, and the day I traded my fifty seven Chevy rag top to it, which proves I was a real Einstein, I had scooted the bench seat all the way back in order to accommodate my six foot four inch frame. When I picked her up on Saturday afternoon she got in the car, and as I was backing out of her drive, she asked if I could move the seat forward since her feet didn't even reach the floorboard. So being the gentleman I was, I said sure, I'd be glad to. Her house was on top of a hill and as we started off down the hill, I reached under the front of the seat for the lever to move the seat forward. I pulled the lever and the seat wouldn't move. Evidently it had frozen in the track and was stuck. So I started jerking with my feet and buck jumping to move the seat. Lord, what happened next is awful to even think about to this day. In my effort to get that seat to move, I broke wind like a pack mule. Yes, that's right. Right in front of her and God, I cracked a flobert. If I had been in possession of a cyanide tablet I would have bitten that sucker instantly. But all I could do was roll down the window and tell her I heard a noise in one of the wheel bearings. She never let on like she even heard it. You could have lit a whole pack of cigarettes off my face. How awful. Years later I mentioned it, and she said, "Had I heard it, I would have said something." I told her she would have been in an accident too, because I would have opened the door and jumped out, never to be seen or heard from again.

The following year, on July 3rd, we became Mr. and Mrs. Kenneth and Linda Croslin, and as of this writing we are into our fortieth year together. Just think, if she'd had keener ears and fewer allergies, we may never have stayed together!

Lost in the Masses
Steve
1969

I'm not sure when it began statewide that the small county schools were consolidated into one or two huge high schools per county. In Warren County, after the 67-68 school year, the Alvaton High School became a grade school and the junior high and high school students became part of Warren Central High School. I'm sure there were many reasons for consolidation from a monetary standpoint that made sense in doing this. There are also some things that were given up that hurt some students. I remember Alvaton at a time when you knew just about every child that went there from first grade through the senior class. You became friends with all your classmates as well as most of your teachers. It was just so much more personal. My brother Steve was an honor student at Alvaton and the last five years he went to school there, he had perfect attendance. His freshman year at Central he broke the string of perfect attendance and missed a few days. Sometime during his sophomore year he really broke down. Our Momma got a phone call from one of his teachers one evening and she wanted to know how Steve was doing. Momma said he was doing fine as far as she knew and why was she asking? His teacher said, "Well, Mrs. Croslin, he hasn't been to school in twenty six days." Momma was floored to say the least and she tried to control herself when she asked Steve what was going on. Did he miss all those days? He confessed that he had indeed. She started to cry, which is the very worst thing any of us ever wanted to see. He told her he had been working for some of the local farmers hauling hay in order to buy her an air conditioner so she could sleep better during really hot weather and he actually did buy one a little later. She talked him into going back to school.

His first day back to school, his homeroom teacher asked him to stay after class and to meet him in the gym. Steve went on to the gym and waited for him. When the teacher showed up he had a paddle and told him he would have to take a lick with the paddle for every day he had missed since it was school policy. Steve told him he wasn't going to take any licks with a paddle for missing school days. He would make up the work or do whatever it took but he was not going to be whipped and he walked out of high school never to return again.

In 1990 Steve went through an adult education class at work, and then he took the G.E.D. test which he passed on the first try and got his high school equivalency diploma. I'm not sure where the problem began, but in a school the size of Alvaton, there's not a chance in the world he would have gone that long without someone calling our Momma to see what was wrong with him. With an attendance record like he had, his missing school would have been caught on to in less than a week.

Momma's Last Move
Julia
1969

In nineteen sixty nine we were living in
Alvaton at the Thurman Pearson place. My
Momma paid fifty dollars a month rent, and for a
house without a bathroom that was pretty high.
She had never had a bathroom in the house
except one time at the Fizer farm and we only
lived there a year. My sister Barbara and her
husband Jack were looking for a few acres to
buy in Warren County. They found a little baby
farm in the Anna community with a four room
house on it. Jack checked it out and they
decided to buy it all and then sell Momma the
house and a garden spot. He went to the Federal
Home Administration and found out Momma
was eligible for a loan under the conditions that
the house had to have a bathroom and meet a
minimum amount of square footage. They told
Momma about the deal and it scared her to
death to think she would owe for a house.
Including the new bathroom, and a living room
and kitchen the house was going to cost twelve
thousand dollars and the payments would be
forty eight dollars per month. Wow, she was
going to have her own seven room house with a
bath, and the payments were going to be less
than she had been paying for rent. But our
Momma was a worrier. She said, "Why, I'll never
live long enough to pay for it," but she did by
several years. She was so proud of her house
and we were proud for her because she deserved
a few nice things in her life. It was a pretty little

white house with green shutters and a white picket fence around it with rambling roses growing on it. She had worked like a dog all her married life, lived through the Great Depression, raised eleven kids, became a widow at forty nine years old, survived cancer, and helped raise two grandchildren. She did all that without ever complaining or feeling sorry for herself that we knew of.

We had some fine times working on her house over the years. I remember once we put new shingles on the roof and painted the entire house all in one day. All her children and their wives and husbands worked on it. My brother in law Jack grilled hot dogs, hamburgers and chicken for everybody and the girls made the potato salad, desserts, and the rest of the goodies. We worked like a bunch of towheads and had a wonderful time. Momma, with stooped shoulders, would walk around and around the house, her hands behind her back taking it all in and just shaking her head in wonder at all the goings on. At least we all came in handy for once anyway.

Momma enjoyed her house so much because she had never had a place before that she could call her own, to decorate it, and do with whatever she wanted. It was truly her time to live in comfort and ease because it was her mansion here on earth. But I know she had a mansion awaiting her in heaven. We lost Momma in ninety seven due to a stroke, at the age of eighty five years and one month and she died with her children gathered around her bed. Her children were there with her until she took her last breath.

You know, when you lose a parent that has been very, very ill and their quality of life is gone, we hate giving them up of course, but we'd have to be very selfish to want to hold on to them longer in that condition. That has been our thoughts, especially when we know Momma's last move was to a much, much better place.

One Hot Dude and One Cool Chick
Sid
1970

Linda and I got married July 3rd, nineteen seventy at the same little country church where we are both members now. If you went to the Daily News archives and checked the weather for that date, you would find it was terribly hot. It was in the upper nineties. Our little church at that time had no air conditioning and a metal roof. We got married at 3:30 in the afternoon, and Lord was it hot in there. As we stood there during the ceremony I had sweat dripping off my chin. She was as cool as could be and beautiful too. We had only been married two minutes and she was already feeling sorry for me. When we turned to face the crowd, it looked like I had wet my pants. They were wet down to my knees, and I think it was all perspiration. Not certain, but I think it was. I told you I was one hot dude! I was also one nervous dude. That's the only time I've ever gotten married, and only the second wedding I had ever been to. I was the best man at the wedding of the two friends that got Linda and me together. I've made two perfect choices in my lifetime. Getting right with God, and asking Linda to marry me. I think I'm one up on her. She has helped me to believe in myself in so many ways. She encouraged me to get my G.E.D. and attend some college classes. I would never have been able to advance in my work without the G.E.D. She has been my rock through lots of hard times. We have three wonderful children who are all successful, and have never given us one problem. When they were small, she quit work and stayed home with them. When she first quit work, I was afraid we might really have a hard time financially, but we got by even better than when she worked. Our daughter remembers coming home from school and smelling homemade cookies. I remember coming home from work and smelling chicken frying and two or three vegetables cooking and biscuits or corn bread. Sounds good huh? We always had good home cooked meals and we always ate together. All three kids remember afternoons sitting in her rocking chair with her, eating snacks and watching children's shows on T.V. or outside playing. I believe that's the way kids should be raised today.

Since we married, we've only moved four times, and the last move we made was thirty four years ago. I got my fill of moving while growing up as a sharecropper's kid.

Back to School
Sid
1973

Throughout America, students are dropping out of high school at an alarming rate. This has always been a problem and continues to be so. Why is it happening, and what can we do about it? I've always believed not every one is cut out for college, yet the entire curriculum is steered that way in high school. We spend an exorbitant amount of time studying Shakespeare and Algebra. That's wonderful if you plan to be an actor or an engineer, but how many of our children plan to do that? In reality, most young people make their living working in factories, small businesses, and agriculture-related jobs. In most schools, there is a certain group of kids that fall into the cracks, and if you stay in the cracks long enough you will eventually fall through them. There should be more time spent on general studies that will help a person get through this life. How many kids when they graduate know how to balance a checkbook, establish a budget and live within it, repair a leaking faucet in their home, or the many other things we really need to know in order to be self sufficient and productive citizens?

I believe our children should be challenged to learn more, but in reality, unless we offer studies that fit the needs of all the children, some numbers of them are simply overwhelmed and lose hope and if you lose hope you sometimes just quit.

My entire family always liked doing things together. Someone was always getting a new idea for a little adventure. One Sunday we were visiting our Momma and someone mentioned they had heard about adult education classes being offered at night at each school in Warren County. I don't remember which one of us started it, but pretty soon we were discussing going back to school. Before we knew it, Elizabeth, Jeanne, Tommy, Steve and I had decided we would give it a try. Of eleven children, only two had graduated from high school. We started going to Richardsville Elementary each Tuesday night to study for the G.E.D. test. After a couple of classes, the teacher told me he thought I could pass the test since it hadn't been that long since I left school. I went to one more night session and Jeanne felt like she could pass the test by this time as well. We signed up to take the test at W.K.U. We both took it the same day and we both passed it. I'm sorry now that we took it before all of us were ready for it. Elizabeth and Tommy I don't believe ever went back for any more night classes after that. I'm sure we would all have received our G.E.D. if we had stayed together. That's just one more thing in my life I wish I could do over.

Tough and Troubled
Robert
1939--1979

Rheumatic fever is an inflammatory disease than can develop from such things as strep throat and also from scarlet fever if inadequately treated. It's quite rare in the United States and other developed countries. It can cause heart problems as well as severe inflammation of the joints, and it usually affects children from five to fifteen but can also affect infants and adults.

My brother Robert was diagnosed with Rheumatic Fever when he was twelve or thirteen years old. He had a severe case and it pretty much left him crippled for a couple of years. There probably weren't very good treatments for it in the early fifties. We lived at the Fiser place where we milked dairy cattle, took care of beef cattle, and raised tobacco. Mr. Fiser owned a plumbing company in Bowling Green, and just about every week he would drive out to the farm to see his cattle. They were his hobby, and it also got him out of the office for a little while. On nice warm sunny days that spring, Robert would hobble out on the porch to sit in the sunshine. I guess he got some relief from the painful swollen joints. One day while he was on the porch, Mr. Fiser drove in the driveway to look at his cattle. He said hello to Robert and asked him why wasn't he out running and ripping on such a nice day. He told him if he could that's exactly what he'd be doing, but since he couldn't walk very well he'd just stay on the porch. Mr. Fiser asked him what was wrong with him and Robert told him about the rheumatic fever, and that he just wasn't able to do anything. The old man said, "I'll tell you what I'll do, Robert. If you come down to the shop I'll pay you a dollar an hour to keep the place swept up and clean." I suppose by this time Robert had pretty much given up, but a dollar an hour was big money to a fifteen year old crippled boy in nineteen fifty five and he said he would like to give it a try. So he started sweeping the store and shop and it wasn't too long before he started to improve in his ability to get around. After a few months Mr. Fiser started sending him out on the service trucks as a plumber's helper and he continued to improve. He was interested in what they were doing and he was a quick learner and a hard worker.

I think it would be safe in saying that old man saved Robert's life by getting him out of a chair and up on his feet. It probably strengthened his heart as well as the rest of his body. By the time he was twenty he was strong as a mule and handsome as could be. He remained healthy for about seven or eight years before the disease resurfaced as rheumatoid arthritis. He slowly began to be bothered by it and it continued to get worse as time went by. His joints would swell to twice their normal size and the pain was terrible but he never gave in to it. He worked every day as a plumber, out in all kinds of weather, crawling under houses across frozen ground to thaw or repair ruptured water lines, in frozen ditches repairing broken water mains, and never complained. Robert had a lot of our Momma and Daddy in him. I imagine he also knew if he quit working, he would only get worse faster. I've seen his fingers, ankles, knees and elbows swollen to twice their normal size but he kept going. It was heart breaking to see him so young and so miserable with the pain.

There was a medication they called Gold Shots that really helped him but only lasted about a year and you could only take two of them. After that he couldn't get any relief from the pain, so he began to drink and progressively got more and more dependent on alcohol. I don't know if alcohol helped or just made him not care. At any rate, he eventually developed cirrhosis of the liver which took his life at the age of thirty nine years old. While he was in the hospital the last few days before he died, I visited him every day and talked with him and he never seemed bitter or angry even though he knew he didn't have many days to live. I'll regret as long as I live the fact that I never told him I loved him. In all the time I knew him I never did tell him that. Our family just didn't do that except with our mother. Robert died knowing all his brothers and sisters loved him but he never heard us say it. I made myself a promise that would never happen again and it hasn't, but how can something as simple as saying I love you to a family member be so difficult? I can take some comfort from knowing that it's better to show someone you love them than to just say you love them. Anyone can say "I love you" whether they mean it or not.

I'm sure there were some people that saw Robert as just another drunk but those same people never knew the constant pain he felt every day. They may have been the type that missed work due to a hangnail but he never did. He worked right up until the last month he lived. He was an inspiration to me and I loved him!

Pappy's Old Fiddle
Sid
1984

My Momma's daddy, Jim White, was an old time fiddle player and from what I've heard over the years he could really play. He played for community events, house parties, and political gatherings. He would walk or ride a horse or mule to these gatherings. After Grandpa White died, Grandma moved in with my Aunt Sarah. After Grandma passed away, Sarah wound up with Grandpa's old fiddle. Now Aunt Sarah was never musically inclined, nor did she have any children to leave this old fiddle to after she died. She kept the fiddle for about forty years. I suppose since I played music most of my life, she felt like I should have it. So she called my Momma and told her to have me come by her house, since she wanted to see me about something. So I went by Momma's house, picked her up and took her with me to visit her sister. When we got there we visited for a long time and she never mentioned what she wanted to see me about. I guess she was so wound up chatting with Momma she had just forgotten about asking me to come over. When we were getting ready to leave, I said "Aunt Sarah, you said you wanted to see me about something." She said, "Why yes, I'd plumb forgot it. Just hold on there a minute, I'll be right back." She went in the other room and when she came back, she had Grandpa's old fiddle case under her arm. She opened the case and there it was. I'd heard about it all my life but that was the first time I had ever seen it. The strings were rusty, the bow hairs were all broken, but the fiddle itself was in pretty good condition. It probably hadn't been touched since Grandpa last played it. She said, "I want you to have this fiddle since you play music and I know you'll take care of it. It's really a good fiddle! It's a Briggs and Stratton!" Now you'd have to have known my Aunt Sarah to appreciate that. What she meant to say was she thought it was a Stradivarius, which is probably the most sought after violin in the world, and there were never but a few made. An original Stradivarius would bring mega bucks today most likely. I could find no evidence of any kind of what make fiddle this is. There are no markings or labels at all in it or on it. I suspect it was sold by Sears and Roebuck. Sears was known for selling pretty good instruments at an affordable price, somewhere around thirty dollars back in the thirties or forties. At any rate it is a priceless heirloom and will always stay in the family. I gave it to my youngest son Kevin because he is a really good fiddle player and will also take good care of it and keep it. I have a feeling Grandpa would be proud, knowing his old fiddle is still in the family and still being played by one of his great grandchildren. I know I am!

Back from the Dead
Julia
1993

My family has always kept in touch with each other and especially with our Momma. Nearly every Sunday afternoon, several of us wound up at Momma's house to visit with her and with each other. In the winter time we grownups usually sat around and talked while the kids played board games. But in the warmer months we were usually outside at the picnic table drinking iced tea or coffee.

One day in particular, probably in April, we were all there at once and some of the kids wanted to play softball in the garden spot next to the house. It hadn't been worked up yet, so we got up a ball game. Everybody was playing except Momma, and she had been watching. She had gotten up and gone inside to do something, and her cat she called McCallister was sitting on the picnic table enjoying the sunshine. The picnic table was right along the third base line and there sat the cat, with her front paws drawn up in under her and she was blinking her eyes real slow and just about asleep. I'll never forget what happened next! My brother Billy was getting too lame to run very fast so he had to really clobber a ball in order to get around the bases. He was at bat and he hit a line drive foul ball that hit Momma's old cat right upside the head. Off the picnic table she rolled dead as a mackerel. Only the tip of her tail wiggled a little and that was it. God, we knew we were in trouble for killing Momma's old cat, so I decided to get rid of the evidence. I grabbed McCallister by the tail and ran down behind her house and wound her up like a sling and threw her way down in the woods. I hated doing that but I would have hated it worse to tell Momma we had killed her cat. Everybody was sworn to secrecy about the demise of McCallister. We broke up the ball game and went back to drinking our tea and coffee. One by one we all remembered something we had to do at home, so it wasn't long before everyone had left. I felt terrible about the cat since Momma loved her company so, and it was the first cat she had ever really taken to.

I, my wife and children were down there a few days later visiting Momma. We were making small talk and Momma said, "Kenny, I don't know what's happened to McCallister." I acted surprised when she said it and I said, "Aw Momma, you know how cats are, they'll just sometimes take off and you never see them again." She said, "No, she's still here, but her head is all swelled up and she's cross-eyed." There was a chill ran down my back like a half dozen little tiny bulldozers. I said, "Momma, that cat must have got bitten by a copperhead or some other poisonous snake." She said, "You're probably right." Eventually McCallister's head did get back to its normal size but her eyes never did straighten up. I bet she would have scratched you all over if you'd try to set her down on that picnic table again after her encounter with that missile. We never confessed to being responsible for what happened to her old cat. Grandpa always said,"Leave a sleeping dog lie" and we figured it must hold true for cats as well.

The Rock
Sarah Elizabeth
1931- 1993

Elizabeth was the oldest of Phillip and Julia's eleven children. She was born when Momma was only eighteen years old and they kind of grew up together. She was a rather large woman, big boned, big hearted and beautiful in every way. She had the most beautiful big brown eyes you ever saw and several of her nieces have those same eyes. She was knee deep in love with her family and would have fought a Grizzly bear over any of us. She had a wonderful sense of humor and was so much like our Daddy it was spooky. She looked like him and had his personality as well. She loved a joke better than anybody and knew a million of them.

Elizabeth probably had to work too hard as a child, maybe even to the point of not really having a childhood of her own, but she never complained once that I ever heard about and was just like a mother to every one of her brothers and sisters. After our Daddy died, I'm sure there were times she slipped Momma a little money on the side to help out although she would never have mentioned it and would have told Momma not to. I loved her like a mother as did all the rest of us. She was the one you could go to if you needed to talk, or if you needed some help. She was always there for us. She would also get on your case hot and heavy if she thought you needed it, and we always needed it. She was as proud of our accomplishments as if we were her own kids. Elizabeth was the rock in our family and every one of us knew it.

Our nickname for her was "Scoop," because she knew everybody and who they married, who they were kin to, and just about anything else you needed to know about them I guess. She had a memory like an elephant and was never at a loss for words. She was smart as a whip.

I made her really mad at me only one time as far as I know. One Saturday I stopped by her house to say hello and found her outside in the back yard hanging out clothes to dry. It was August and hot as blazes, so I offered her a little tip. I said Sis, if you'd hang up a pair of your drawers first, you could stand in the shade and hang the rest of them out. She came out from behind that clothes line like a Grizzly bear and for a minute she had murder in those big brown eyes. She said, "Listen you little turd, if that's all you came over here for you can just leave right now." It's strange how something can sound so cute and witty one minute and so hateful the next. Needless to say I spent the next few minutes apologizing to her and saying how sorry I was for saying that. She stared at me a minute and said, "Alright butt head, let's go in and have a cup of coffee," and that was the end of it.

Speaking of coffee, I've never seen but one other person that loved coffee as much as she did, and that was my brother in law Jerry Runner, although he stopped just short of her. As soon as she stepped foot in her house after work she made a pot of coffee. She never owned a drip coffee maker as far as I know. She said it was best made in a percolator and she couldn't wait for the coffee to perk. She would put a pinch of raw coffee in her lip like snuff till the coffee was ready to drink. As far as I know Jerry never stooped to that level.

There's no telling how many young people Elizabeth helped to get jobs at the Derby or what is now called Fruit of the Loom. She didn't think twice about putting her neck on the line for someone that she knew needed a job, but like I said, she knew everybody and just about everything about them. And you would have done whatever it took to not let her down. She worked at the Derby forty three years after lying about her age to get a job. They found out about her little fib and fired her, only to tell her to come back as soon as she turned eighteen. On her eighteenth birthday she went back and they kept their word. She went back to work the very next day. Of course the couple of months she worked illegally didn't count in those forty three years, but the money she made sure did.
 After she and Kenneth Mitchell married in forty eight there weren't many jobs to be had in Warren County, so they moved to Indianapolis to try to find work. They did find jobs, but were never really satisfied living there. Elizabeth told me about living in an upstairs apartment that didn't have air conditioning and it was so hot they couldn't sleep, so they took turns sitting in the open window to cool while the other one slept. It's a wonder one of them didn't go to sleep and fall out the window. They only stayed a couple of months before missing home and

family so bad they decided to return to Kentucky. They did get to see the Indy 500 while they were there so I guess it was worth the trip.

Just when we had all decided they were not going to have any children, surprise, surprise they announced they were expecting. They had been married eleven years when Jennifer Renee was born. No need to rush anything. And guess what, eight years later they had twins. Now how about that? Phillip and Phyllis were the first twins in our family and created quite a bit of excitement. Funny, but a new baby never got to be old hat in our family. We loved them all!

We had family get-togethers several times a year and almost always there was music involved. Elizabeth's favorite song was the "Sloop John B," a huge hit by The Beach Boys, and she always wanted me to sing it for her, and I was glad to do it. For some reason I always thought it strange that she would like that song. People in her age group usually were pure country music lovers, but Sis was progressive in her thinking and pretty hip, come to think about it.

She also loved Braves baseball, and watched every game they played if it was on TV. After she got sick, that was a real source of entertainment for her and Kenneth. It helped pass the time. She would have loved to have seen them win the World Series in ninety five, but all the series losses they endured would have hurt.

Not many days go by that I don't think of Elizabeth and what she meant to me and the rest of us. She had a spirit in her that was contagious to all of us and I loved her for it. I loved her for a thousand reasons and still miss her badly!

I'll see you later Sis!

Green Biscuits
Sid
1994

Julia Louise Croslin could have been a
very famous person if someone had helped her
open her own restaurant. She was a wonderful
cook. Any thing she made was delicious and also
very appetizing to look at as well. She could
make everyday foods melt in your mouth. Right
now I would give a hundred dollars for a meal
she cooked and feel like I got a terrific deal. She
could also make the most delicious pies and
cakes you ever tasted. She took pride in her
meals in the taste and appearance. She taught
all the girls to cook just like her and one or two
of the boys even do very well in the kitchen. I
don't happen to be one of them though. My
expertise falls more in the line of tasting. I can't
cook a lick but I can tell when someone else is
good at it.

A few years ago, my wife, a nurse, was
working at a local doctor's clinic, and it was
winter time during the cold and flu season. All
the patients that called in to see the doctor were
seen after the regularly scheduled patients were
finished and she was always later getting home
that time of year. I got an idea I would cook
supper and have it ready when she got home.
That was so very noble of me, but I didn't know
how to cook. Now if you can't cook, you sure
better know someone that can or you might
possibly do some one in that you love. So I called
Momma and asked her how to make biscuits

since I had decided to have breakfast foods for supper. She asked me what in the world did I want to know how to make biscuits for since she knew Linda was a good cook. I told her my plan and she seemed quite pleased that I would even consider cooking a meal. She gave me explicit instructions on how to make biscuits and I felt my confidence growing that I could actually pull this off. I had called Linda at work to get an approximate time when she might be home since I wanted everything to be ready just as she got home. When the time seemed right I flew in to cooking like I knew what I was doing. Nothing to this cooking! Anybody could do it if they had half sense and a little want to in their blood. Now I'm not going to brag too much but it all came off pretty well. My wife thought she had gotten the wrong house when she walked in and our supper was on the table. I hadn't bothered with candle light since our three kids were there and breakfast foods and candle light doesn't really go together. The eggs and bacon were good, and the biscuits were far, far better than I had even hoped for. I got rave reviews from Linda and the kids and I couldn't wait to call Momma and tell her how good it all was.

As I was dialing the phone to call Momma to tell her all about it and how good it turned out, I had an idea pop into my head to mess with her just a little. As soon as she realized it was me she couldn't wait to ask how the biscuits turned out. I said well, they tasted pretty good but why would they have turned green? I heard her suck in her breath and she got quiet. She could just see three poor little kids, their bellies all swollen, tongues hanging out of their mouths and eyes rolled back in their heads, dead as Aunt Mabel's dog from eating green biscuits. Finally, she said,"Kenneth Roger, what in the world did you put in those biscuits? I told you exactly how to do it!" I saw this was getting way out of hand and her being an old lady I decided she'd suffered enough already so I confessed I'd been lying about the green biscuits. I heard her breathe a sigh of relief and then she gave me a going over for scaring her that way. After a bit she finally saw the humor in it and we had a good laugh. I loved hearing my Momma laugh!

It's Your Move
Jeanne and Julia
1995

My sister Jeanne moved back home with us after she was divorced. She had tuberculosis when she was in her late teens and spent three years in the T.B. Sanitarium in Riverside, outside of Bowling Green. She had married a guy she met while she was there. He was a never do well kind of man and he left her with two young children to raise. She was cured of T.B. but never was a very strong person after that. She never left our home after that and Momma and Daddy were able to provide a home for her and her two boys.

Years later after we had all married and left home it was just her and Momma, which turned out to be a blessing. They were able to take care of one another and it was mutually beneficial for them both. After Momma retired and they spent all day every day together there were times they got on each other's nerves, but for the most part they got along well. They would however argue about the most mundane things you could imagine, like who married who in 1936, or what was the name of the guy that played Tarzan. But the best one they would have is "Who's going to make the pie?" Momma and Jeanne were both excellent cooks whether it was just every day home cooking or world class pies and cakes and the like. They would start off by one of them saying, "Boy, wouldn't a good chocolate pie taste good right about now." The other one would come back with, "Well, you make a better pie than I do so you make one." The other would always counter with "Yeah, I probably do but I made the last one." It would get plumb ridiculous, as this might go on for hours. It was like a chess match between Bobby Fisher and Boris Spasski. They each were as stubborn as two Missouri mules and all this time their appetites were being whetted as sharp as a razor's edge. Finally, one of them would give in to making the pie because they were so hungry for one or they just plain got tired of arguing about it. While the loser would be whipping up a pie, the other would set back and bask in her glory of out-arguing the other. The loser always knew they would live to argue another day. What was so funny about this is when the pie finally came out of the oven by this time they had lost all self control and would try to eat it before it cooled properly resulting in burned lips and tongues. "To the victor belongs the spoils" they always said.

Our mother died in 97 and Jeanne in 98. Jeanne was never the same after Momma died and I believe she just gave up when there was no one left to challenge her in an argument!

Just Plumb Worn Out
Julia
1996

If you were raised up on a farm in
Kentucky in the first part of the 20th century,
you knew hard work. Whether you were a man
or woman it didn't matter, you worked. My
Momma worked hard before she married and
even harder after she married. If you wanted to
survive you worked. There were no free meals.
My Momma and Daddy married in 1929 when
Momma was only 17 years old. They started a
family right away, and by the time the
Depression had really settled in, they already
had two children. Every day was a work day
except Sunday, Thanksgiving, and Christmas.
Momma worked in the fields alongside Daddy,
washed their clothes on a washboard and
cooked three meals a day, as well as took care of
the kids. She did all this with no modern
conveniences, no electricity, and no running
water in the house. It wasn't that Momma and
Daddy were all that different from other folks of
that era either. If you ask someone that had
lived through those Depression years, they
usually just shake their heads and say it was
hard on everybody. My Momma did all that and
raised eleven kids. We always had enough to eat
and clothes to wear, because they made every
lick count. We always put up our own meat,
raised a huge garden and Momma canned all
summer. We ate pinto beans by the truck load
and potatoes by the bushel, and never got tired
of them. I'm still not tired of them and I could

eat anything now I want, but I still had rather have them than almost anything you could offer me. And guess what, we ate healthy. What would be considered unhealthy today was healthy then because we weren't a bunch of couch potatoes. We worked all that off. Aha, there's that word again. Work, now there's a four letter word lots of people hate hearing today. It's funny but I run a lawn and garden equipment repair shop, and some people that have a lawn the size of a postage stamp and a riding lawn mower that will mow an acre in thirty minutes, are the same ones that are overweight, out of shape or go to the gym and pay money to work out. Go figure!

A few years ago, when Momma was eighty four years old and had survived colon cancer in her seventies, with shoulders stooped, arthritis in her joints and diabetes, she was still doing her own house work. One morning while I was at work, I was thinking about her so I called and asked her how she was doing. She said, "Oh Kenny, by the time I get up, cook my breakfast, wash the dishes, make my bed, do a couple loads of laundry, and run the sweeper, I'm just plumb worn out." I said, "Momma, how many people do you know that are younger than you are that can do half that much?" She said, "Well I know, but it just bothers me." Oh, if we all had her spirit!

The Purest Chip Off the Old Block
Tommy
2011

Of all seven boys Phillip and Julia had, I
believe Tommy to be the most like our Daddy in
every way you can think of. He has Daddy's
looks, personality, wit, and charm. He can talk a
poor cat off a bowl of cream. He is good at all the
things Daddy was good at and bad at the things
Daddy was bad at. He loves to talk, joke, trade,
fish, hunt, and laugh. I could go on and on. His
two most favorite things to do are fishing and
trading. I can usually hold my own in fishing
with him but he would have everything but my
socks if I tried trading with him. He has an eye
for a deal and he never trades for something
unless he already has a place for it. He keeps
the ball rolling so to speak. He is always full of
surprises like the time he traded for an
accordion. Now what would a man that doesn't
play music and isn't even interested in learning
want an accordion for? Well, at this writing, it is
in my attic. I don't even remember what I traded
him for it. I never wanted an accordion and don't
know the first thing about one. See what I mean?
Maybe someday, I'll catch him gone from home
and leave it on his front porch with a note from
Joe the Gypsy, telling him I hope he enjoys it
and never to part with it.

Daddy was never a worrier and neither is
Tommy. He just does his thing, takes one day at
a time and is a happy man. Tommy has had a
heart attack, and cancer and he has overcome

221

both of them. He does a much better job of taking care of himself these days than he used to.

Tommy, like Daddy, had a problem with alcohol. They were a little different in that Daddy would get loaded a couple of times a year, but it was usually just a one day thing. Tommy on the other hand, once he started drinking, usually drank till he got past going. Then he would go for several months before falling off the wagon. Years ago he went to an alcohol abuse treatment center. The lady that was interviewing him asked him if he drank all the time. He said, "No, I take it by spells." "What do you mean?" she asked him. "Well," he said, "I drink till I have a spell, then I stop." They both cracked up, and then he left. He stopped drinking about fifteen years ago without any earthly help. He had known for years that he needed to stop drinking. I guess he just finally decided he wanted to.

I've always loved him and today he is one of my very best friends. While writing this story, I've been trying to think of something he has that I could trade a good accordion to!

That's Bad Luck
Phillip

Daddy was a pretty bright fellow on just
about anything you care to mention. He did a lot
of reading and studying of things, and was
always curious to know more. He didn't believe
in ghosts or spooks or the supernatural for the
most part. He did however believe you could
bring some things on yourself by being ignorant,
and this is certainly true. I guess the proper
word that best describes Daddy would be to say
he was superstitious. If you were traveling in a
car and a black cat ran across the road in front
of you, you had two options. You could turn
around and find an alternate route, or draw
an "X" on the seat with your finger and say
"damn it." Either one was an effective antidote
but the "X" saved time and money in gas.
You could get your head noogied for opening an
umbrella in the house. He thought that was
extremely dumb since you shouldn't need one
open in the house to begin with. Evidently, he
had forgotten about the night I was born and the
steamboat biscuits the following morning.
Anybody that would walk under a ladder if
someone was on it was considered to be asking
for it. Anybody could drop a hammer while
working on a ladder and knock you silly as a
goose. He didn't consider that superstition, just
being smart.

If you really wanted to set him off, you'd
go out one door and come back in another. He
would just look at you with disdain as if you had

just climbed out from under a cow pile. I've found myself under his gaze many times and it wasn't a really good feeling. You never laid a hat on the bed, either, for that was a certain sign of death for a loved one. If you were to ask Daddy if he was superstitious, he'd tell you, "No, I just don't like taking chances."

Through it All
The Family
1910-2011

It has taken one hundred and one years to write this book! One heartache at a time, one tear at a time, one laugh at a time, but only three months to put it all down on paper. Many things have resurfaced in my memory since I first put pen to paper. Many poignant events had gotten lost somewhere in the daily grind of holding down a job, raising a family and all the other things that fill up a lifetime and tend to obscure important moments that shape you and truly define who you are. Not many people keep a diary, and even if they did, they might fail to recognize and record the little things that happen that can become so very crucial to us later on. Thank God my family members have good memory and memories that I was able to draw upon in the writing of this book. As we sat around a dining room table and discussed the past events in our lives, the well of information turned from a trickle to a gusher as we talked. While one of us might remember only part of a story, another would remember a different part and between the seven of us, we were able to piece together the entire event with about ninety nine point nine percent accuracy, and that's pretty close for a Croslin!

We were so very fortunate to have had parents that loved us and nurtured us through tough times as children and later on as adults with an entirely different set of problems. None of us remember being held and cuddled and loved on every day, but all of us knew we were loved unconditionally, and there was no end to what our parents would have done for us in times of trouble.

Throughout my Momma's life as a sharecropper's wife and widow, she lived in approximately forty different houses, but she managed to make every single one of them a home. A home where we knew we were loved and would be cared for. I guess one way to look at it is we put down roots all over Warren County, Kentucky from one end of it to the other. It would have taken one mighty strong wind to have blown us apart from each other.

We would never have known we were poor unless someone had told us, for that was the only standard we had to go by. We were living proof you're not sure of what you're missing if you've never had more than what you have at the moment. Now that is a mouthful to ponder upon. I'm positive there were people around us that had money but no peace of mind, who would have gladly traded places with us, people who had forgotten how to love one another in search of a monetary goal or social standing. Maybe that's what happens when your dreams override your heart. Our goals were much more short term and obtainable, for instance getting through another day with food on the table and clothes on our backs and no one getting hurt or becoming ill. Anything beyond that was just icing on the cake of our lives and to be considered a victory.

We had the ability to hunker down and dig our way out of financial poverty. Although I don't believe any of us are financially wealthy, we are rich in many other ways that far outweigh dollars and cents. Businesses in this country are in trouble because they mismanage during the good times, not the bad, by spending money they don't have, or what's worse, by spending other people's money they wish they had. Almost every day was a lesson in economics when we were growing up and we got used to it.

Our family has always been big on get-togethers. We've always gotten together several times a year like Easter for dinner and egg hunts. We celebrated Daddy's birthday July 2nd, and the 4th of July for an Independence Day picnic. July 17th, we gathered for Momma's birthday dinner. We got together on Thanksgiving and at Christmas for dinners. As a result of those gatherings, our children all know each other, our grandchildren all know each other and when one of them hurts, they all feel the pain. That's what family is all about. We've always known it, and we've always promoted it. That may sound a bit clannish to some folks, but to us it's just being family. Over the years, we have lost parents, two brothers and two sisters. With every loss, we seem to draw a little bit closer and hold on to each other a little bit tighter.
I sincerely hope you're enjoying reading this book, and the healing properties it may contain

within its pages and stories as it reminds you of your own family's troubles and trials. It probably won't be a cure-all, but it might just be a start to something you can finish on your own with a little help from your family!

Home is Wherever our Family Was

When it was time to move on to another place, there was almost always a tinge of sadness associated with leaving. We had usually made some new friends that we hated leaving behind. I don't remember ever leaving behind a girl friend, or at least one that even knew I was alive. Some of the places we lived I wish we could have owned. There was even one place I wish I had owned just so I could burn it to the ground. It was called the Hardcastle place, but we just called it the pneumonia hole! It was the coldest house I have ever spent the night in. I actually saw a bucket of water freeze almost solid while setting within three feet of a red hot stove. I heard it was donated to the Alvaton Volunteer Fire Department to burn for practice. I don't know how they ever got it hot enough to burn. My Momma had to put a hair dryer under the covers in order to get her feet warm enough that she could go to sleep. The poor little old mice used to keep us awake nights while sniffling their little runny noses. Needless to say, we never stayed there long.

My favorite place to live I think, was Mrs. Georgia Willoughby's at Claypool. It sat way back in the woods, in the edge of a clearing and I have many fond memories of living there. I loved hanging out with my Daddy when he was working with his mules and horses. Once in a while he would dress his mules up in the best harness he had, trim their manes, dock their tails and polish their hooves. He had some of the brightest colored tassels of red, yellow, orange and blue he would attach to the haimes. He would wash the old wagon as well. You have all seen young guys spend all day Saturday, washing, waxing, and shining their cars in order to show them off to their friends in town. Well, Daddy was no different with his mules. We would drive them out to Curtis Weaver's store where there was usually a few of his friends there on Saturday afternoon talking and swapping knives and lies. He would swell up with pride if someone commented on what a fine rig he had. I swelled up too, for I was also proud of him and his team. If it had been dry for a pretty good while, the iron rims on the wagon wheels would get loose and could eventually come off. The way to keep this from happening was to drive the wagon out in the pond, getting the wet sticky mud all over the hubs and spokes. This swelled the wood and tightened the rims back up good as new. I loved riding out in the pond with Daddy in the wagon. I thought that was a pretty awesome ride.

I watched Daddy trim the mule's mane with a pair of mule shears and then hang them back up in the gear room. I guess I figured if they made a mule look good, just think what they would do for me, so I got the shears down and right down the middle of my head I went, just snipping away. It was an awful looking head I took to the house, and Momma had a fit. She whipped me first, which didn't amount to much, but then Daddy gave me a whipping and it amounted to enough that I had some left over for interest on the next one.

You can go Home again in Memories
Epilogue
2011

Throughout my life I've been an avid reader of books. I've read everything from Louis L'Amour paperbacks to Pearl S. Buck. I read every book in the Alvaton library and the good ones twice. Textbooks just never held the same interest to me as a good novel, with my favorite being books such as Jessie Stuart's non-fiction works. For some reason, I just never considered trying to write a book before now. I've written a couple of hundred country songs, and even recorded an album of my songs in Nashville, back in the early nineties. One of my songs went to number two among the Independent Record labels, and the top fifty in the major charts. It came to a point where I had to make a decision-- quit my day job of more than twenty years, buy a tour bus and hit the road without my family, or give up the music business. That was more sacrifice than I was willing to make for a career in music. A wife and three children were worth much, much more to me. I've never once regretted that decision.

You've all heard the old saying "You can never go home again" and in a physical sense maybe that's true, for the chain that ties you to home has been broken, and until we can turn back time, it will remain broken. I have found however, you can go home again in memories. Every chapter in this book has taken me home again to some place or point in time. I'd be much less than honest if I told you I'd like to do it all over again, for it was just too hard the first time around. They say hard times don't last, and maybe for some people they don't, but the memories of them sure have hung on for me. Fortunately for me, I have many more good memories than bad ones of growing up poor. Every story in this book evokes memories that were almost dead to me. Oh, the main topic was clear enough, but the little circumstances that surrounded it had just gone fuzzy till we began rehashing things amongst ourselves. Since I began this book, I have revisited, in my memory, the old places where we have lived. I can remember so many things about each one, things like flower beds in the yard, left by a former share cropper's wife, trees in the yards with tire swings, and initials of sweethearts carved into them. Believe it or not, I can even remember the wallpaper prints in a couple of the houses and that's been over fifty years ago. I'm sure there are some things I should remember that I don't, and maybe I don't really want to.

I know my older siblings had it even tougher than me from a standpoint of hard work and doing without things but I had enough of it to not want to return to it for sure! If you ask me, I'd tell you I'm living the good life right now. My wife of forty years is my best friend and soul mate. My children are all successful and have given us three wonderful grandchildren. We have a nice home, car, and truck, and can go anywhere we want, any time we want, eat anything we want, whenever we want it. In "the good old days" as we hear them called so often, I had none of those things. So I'll just be very satisfied with what I have right now! But I will say this; I wouldn't take a million dollars for the memories of those "growing up" years. Through those memories I can go back home, any time I want to!

13437058R00136

Made in the USA
Lexington, KY
02 February 2012